HOW FAR DOWN DARE I DRINK?

How Far Down Dare I Drink?

Promises Greater Than Dreams

More Sermons

By
HORTON DAVIES

Edited By
David Cain and Marie-Hélène Davies

Foreword By
Leslie Carl Smith

WIPF & STOCK · Eugene, Oregon

HOW FAR DOWN DARE I DRINK?
Promises Greater Than Dreams
More Sermons

Copyright © 2014 David Cain and Marie-Hélène Davies. All rights reserved. Except for brief quotations in critical publications or reviews, no part of this book may be reproduced in any manner without prior written permission from the publisher. Write: Permissions. Wipf and Stock Publishers, 199 W. 8th Ave., Suite 3, Eugene, OR 97401.

Wipf and Stock
An Imprint of Wipf and Stock Publishers
199 W. 8th Ave., Suite 3
Eugene, OR 97401

www.wipfandstock.com

ISBN 13: 978-1-62564-563-0

Manufactured in the U.S.A.   04/29/2014

To Horton's children: Christine, Hugh, and Philip,

His grandchildren: Alex, Dorian, Rick, and Jesse,

His present great-grandchildren: Cypress, Han Yun,

And others to come.

Contents

Foreword by Leslie Carl Smith | ix
Acknowledgements | xi

Introduction I: Literary Commentary | 1
Introduction II: How Far Down Dare I Drink? | 17

PART ONE
Responses To Gospel: A Yet More Blazing Certainty

FAITH

The Tide Turned: Transfiguration—Mount of Triumph,
  Mount of Defeat | 33
Death, Getaway of Life Eternal:
  The Adventure of *Analusis* (ἀνάλυσις) | 38
Christian Certainties in an Uncertain World:
  A Colony of Heaven on Earth | 42

HOPE

We Are Saved by Hope: The Victory in His Eyes | 49
Christian Realism:
  Uncontrollable Skidding in the Automobile of Life | 55
Christian Realism:
  Nassau Presbyterian Church, Princeton, April 26, 1959. | 57

LOVE

Communion Address:
  A Cross in the Heart of God—That Crimson Love | 65
The Christian Motive : The Love of Christ Constrains Us | 69

Joy

A Talk on Carols: The Original Merry Christmas | 77
Triple Victory: The Flag Blown Taut | 81
The Two Census Books: Income Tax, Outcome Tax | 85

Responsibility

Communion Address: Glorifying in the Cross | 93
The Christian Sense of Direction: A Pilgrimage from God to God | 99
Advent: Fulfillment and Finality | 103
Burning Bushes and Blackberries:
  Giving, Getting, and Different Pairs of Eyes | 108
The Cloister, and the Hearth, and the Community:
  How Far Down Dare I Drink? | 113

Gratitiude

Harvest Thanksgiving: Gratitude | 123

PART TWO
Cross-Examination: Not from the Comfort of a Pulpit

First Witness: The Mother. Behold the Handmaiden of the Lord | 129
Judas Iscariot: Have You Never Met a Judas? | 133
Caiaphas: Hypocrite as His Soul Deadens | 138
The King—Herod: The Strain of Christ's Silent Scrutiny | 143
Pontius Pilate: He Washes His Hands | 147
The City Counselor, Joseph of Arimathea: A Deserter in Bed | 154
The Soldier—Longinus: You Are the Centurion | 158

PART THREE
Faith and Art: Alive to the Color and Glory of the Universe

Faith and Fine Art: Loving God, Loving Art | 165
The Value of Modern Fiction for Preachers:
  Extra Lives; Extensions of Empathy; Concrete Imagination | 172
Worship and the Renewal of the Church:
  Christian Art. The Holiness of Beauty | 182
Pilgrimage: Eden Lost and Emmaus Found | 189

Foreword

I read—no, I listen to—the sermons of Horton Marlais Davies because he was a kind man.

His sermons speak of the grace he encountered in the living God who, in his grace, became the loving redeemer of the world (and of Horton Davies).

And, Davies's sermons illustrate the benevolence he showed to a new, rather uncertain preacher in town who spoke to him, the church historian, about his anxiety in the pulpit, felt each time he saw in the congregation more than a few of the authors of the books that had been read during his seminary days. Davies answered, "University faculty members do not attend your parish church to hear an academic lecture; they are there to hear the Gospel, to listen to the Good News, and you proclaim that so well."

Not simply Davies the scholar, but Davies the kind scholar.

HOW FAR DOWN DARE I DRINK? This welcome volume of sermons amply shows that central spirit of Horton Davies.

His tenderness toward Mary in "First Witness: the Mother; Behold the Handmaiden of the Lord," does not prevent him from describing the worn, haggard woman at the base of cross, yet the charm and bravery of the young handmaiden shines forth as well. Davies preaches bluntly that "She never understood Jesus." Still, his over-all portrait is that of a girl-woman who is utterly admirable.

Going to the opposite pole in preaching on Judas, Davies says in "Judas Iscariot; Have You Never Met a Judas?" that Judas was called by Jesus to be a follower because Judas had "possibilities of greatness." Davies's closing words on the great betrayer are as kind as Judas could ever have heard, "Judas was great in his passing."

Depth of research. Rich story-telling. Compelling portraits. Clear understanding of the world. Wise understanding of humanity. Solid, humble

Foreword

self-knowledge. All these attributes of Horton Davies are mediated in these sermons through the all-pervasive quality of his kindness.

    The Rev. Dr. Leslie Carl Smith
    Rector Emeritus
    Trinity Church, Princeton
    November 2013

Acknowledgements

After the publication of *Believing*, organized according to the Apostles' Creed, and of *Preaching to a World in Crisis*, which followed the path of Horton Davies's firsthand experience of the troubled world, many of Davies's sermons still remained unpublished. Considering the vividness and qualities of imagination in these sermons, the obvious choice for this third volume co-editor was a long-time student of Horton's and a friend of us both, David Cain, known to me not only for his scholarly research, but also for his involvement with the theatre. Despite a very full schedule as professor, Kierkegaard expert, and editor of many books, Dr. Cain finally gave his expertise to this labor of love, organizing it, and writing its learned introduction and running footnotes. To him and his long-standing friendship I am most indebted. Many thanks are due also to Leslie Smith, who agreed to write the foreword, and with whom Horton had many friendly discussions in mutual appreciation, when Leslie was our rector at Trinity Church, Princeton.

    I, David, particularly wish to thank Cindy Toomey, Office Manager of our Department of Classics, Philosophy, and Religion (CPR) at University of Mary Washington for assistance "above and beyond." Thanks, too, to Carla Bailey, Interlibrary Loan Supervisor, Simpson Library, Mary Washington. She has been a wonderful aide over many years—and is still on the trail of a reference (George MacDonald).

    We also want to thank Baker Library at Dartmouth College, for their media expertise, and willing assistance, Jim Tedrick and Christian Amondson of Wipf and Stock, who readily agreed to publishing the book, Matthew Wimer, who joined the project, Susan Manchester and Christine Pisani for their editing skills.

    We appreciate with wonder the enduring welcome of the Department of Religion, Princeton University, and of Trinity Church, all warming the hearts of widows with the flame of their steady affection. MHD and DC

Introduction I
Literary Commentary

Marie-Hélène Davies

People who are afflicted with the twin passion of preaching and writing will probably agree that each benefits the other. For example, in writing, when you slowly and painstakingly fold a clever crease in syntax, when you layer and lean parallelisms one upon another just so, when you learn to signal your logical connections with sturdy connecting words like *indeed*, *however*, and *for example*, you practice skills that are likely to sneak out when you preach—to your surprise and your hearers' delight.

And similarly preaching can't help but teach you something about writing. You learn to feel the rhythm of the sentence ... You learn to simplify, which is harder than it looks. You learn to write in a whisper, maybe; to romance your readers with a scrap of punctuation—just as you might do with a gesture, or sigh ...[1]

Unlike the sermons of Frederick Buechner, those of Horton Davies were not initially meant to be published, but to be heard. Often conceived under the pressure of the moment, punctuation may not have been of primary concern, and emphasis was often shown with bolding and capitals which have to be changed for publication. It remains that Mr. Maclaren's remarks

---

1. Brian D. Maclaren, "Foreword," Frederick Buechner, *Secrets in the Dark: A Life in Sermons* (San Francisco: HarperCollins, 2006), p. ix.

certainly apply, since Davies was an English major, who, in his youth, had earned the Shakespeare competition prize at Edinburgh, by learning by heart the major part of the bard's work. To this we may add the passion he had for the arts, which makes his delineation of characters, both visual and psychological, all the more vivid and true to life, as we shall see in this particular volume.

As in other volumes, one notes the christological thrust of Davies's sermons; in preaching, in the legacy of Karl Barth [1886–1968], he is not describing but offering God to his congregation, according to what he perceived as its need, whether in his London parish or at various other occasions: graduations, combinations of lecture and preaching invitations, or Westminster Abbey.

Davies is no ostrich. The sermons occasionally reflect on the wretchedness of man, but they are rarely biographical, accusatory, or despondent, in the hope that Christ will help us to become what he wants us to be. The pulpit should serve only Christian truth and its application to the present time, not the ups and downs of the preacher's personal life or beliefs, nor those of his audience of parishioners. But history is present, as always, looming over and darkening the scene, whether it appears as the Second World War, with a sharp attack on the Nazis, or as an allusion to the Vietnam War; or whether in a sociological call for justice, and for human rights and equality for both blacks and women, or concerns for the double-edged welfare state solution to the socioeconomic divide.

Here, in this part of the introduction, we shall limit ourselves to the artistry of the Davies sermons, the devices by which he kept his congregation's attention. We shall pay some particular attention to his capacity for portraits, especially those in the "Cross-Examination" series.

Davies's sermons are firmly grounded in Scripture, from which he derives his exegesis. Most of the sermons in this series are prefaced by one or two biblical texts, mostly from the New Testament and the Acts of the Apostles, but occasionally from the Old Testament—Genesis, Exodus, or Samuel, for instance. But even when the text is not identified as such, the biblical reference is usually there. "Harvest Thanksgiving" starts with Jesus asking his disciples whether they are able to go through the ordeal to come; the opening question in "The Verdict on the Cross" —"What think you of Jesus?" a sermon previously published in *Believing*—could well be the question Pilate would ask of Caiaphas or the crowd.

Introduction I

Although most of the sermons are expository, the "Cross-Examination" series relies mostly on imagination and psychological interpretation. Therefore, as portraits of the characters involved in the Crucifixion drama, they require no biblical quotations as an introduction. Yet Joseph of Arimathea's portrait has the honor of being preceded by reference to the four gospels, a unique instance perhaps devised to assess the historical reality of the character, doubted by some.

There remain the sermons that profess the preacher's personal belief on the role of lore, or art, or literature in church preaching; for these debated topics, it is fit that they should have no biblical reference in order to avoid controversy.

Although the sermons are not plain, Davies mostly adopted the puritan "plain style" in that rhetoric is used only for argumentation and rarely for decoration, as was often the case among the "metaphysical" preachers of the 17th century. The text is interpreted according to the three categories of doctrine, reason, and use, dear to the nonconformists. But following the recent fashion of his time, Davies does not expound on one chapter of the Bible, as these preachers often did. Without using the lectionary dear to the Episcopalians, he chooses the text that best applies to the concerns of the time, and of his congregation, while still remaining faithfully christological.

Relevance to the people was his main concern. In "Harvest Thanksgiving" published in this volume, Davies refers to St. Paul's legacy in this matter:

> St. Paul, because he was a great preacher, had the art of adapting himself to his hearers. When he was at Athens, facing a scholarly audience, he preached a learned sermon about the purposes of God. When he was at Corinth, the great commercial center, where men were mainly concerned with making money, he determined to speak of nothing "save Jesus Christ, and him crucified," to remind them of the vanity of earthly things. Our text was addressed to a very different audience, the simple, unlettered people of Lystra—people so ignorant that they took Paul and Barnabas for gods. So St. Paul chooses as his subject the simplest of all religious themes, the gratitude we owe to God for rains and fruitful seasons, for food and gladness.

The rest of this sermon is a hymn of joyful praise to the creation and the need for wonder and gratitude.

In this volume, we find some examples of the concerns of his congregation: "Triple Victory" celebrates Easter with Londoners in the midst of German bombing, and, like many other sermons of the early period, addresses the anxiety of those whose dear ones are or will be soon in the war. On a lighter note, the graduation sermons address the preoccupations of the three groups participating in the ceremony: parents, young people, and teachers. The preacher acknowledges the relief that graduation brings to the anxiety of all, yes . . . but the teacher resurfaces in urging the graduating class, men and women, to go and serve the world responsibly, according to the lights they have received, thanks to their education. Not fearing to be controversial, Davies discusses in "The Cloister, and the Hearth . . ." the contribution Betty Friedan has made to the advancement of women:

> I think she is right in delineating three stages in the history of the education of women: first, the feminist stage when the pioneers of female education gave women man's education to prove that almost everything a man could do, a mannish woman could do better. The second stage was the more recent feminine mystique stage, when education seemed directed at producing frowsier hausfraus. The third stage will be when women are educated to be full personalities playing a role of leadership in the community, fully the equals of men.

In at least three or four sermons of this series, "A Talk on Carols," "Faith and Fine Art," "The Holiness of Beauty," and "The Value of Modern Fiction for Preachers," Davies, an art-lover, stresses the role of beauty partly to attract the interest of the wealthier part of his Christian congregation. Listen and look at your visionary artists and litterateurs! he says. The Word is incarnate! Praise the tradition of music and beauty of the Christmas season; praise the creators of religious music; praise the visual artists; praise even the relevant atheist or agnostic artists for, whether they recognize it or not, they had been immersed from childhood into the Christian basis of their western civilization! By sensitizing his flock to the religious content of other disciplines of the humanities, he also opens up sensitivities to the religious world outside the confining perimeter of the denominational church building so they will find Judeo-Christian themes in both likely and unlikely places.

Davies speaks to simpler concerns, as in "The Christian Sense of Direction" while saying that these material concerns are not enough to feed the soul:

> What are we working for? An attractive 3 or 4 bedroomed house, centrally heated, with a garage and tool-shop for the husband, and

a shiny kitchen for the wife, with refrigerator, electric-polisher, electric washing and drying, and possibly an automatic dishwasher.

Yet later, he acknowledges the advantages of mass-production, despite its dangers: "so that not only Lord Nuffield, but also Sam Smith can afford the mini-minor, and Dame Margot Fonteyn as well as Molly Smith can buy St Margaret's woolen vests at Marks and Spencer's."

Finally, he appeals to children by anecdotes or by preaching around their own fields of interest: the boredom of listening to a long sermon, or concern for a baby brother's thirst; or joyfully picking berries from the bushes, shepherding with the help of "Doggie thinks—a precursor to our modern Martha television show—making boats out of trees . . .

Indeed Davies is sensitive to the living concerns of his congregation.

SERMONS' BEGINNINGS

To catch the attention of his captive congregation, Davies's sermons have strong beginnings. Surprising anecdotes are some of his favorites, working like parables: the little girl preferring the service music to listening to the Word, in "A Talk on Carols"; holiday plans in "Christian Certainties"; being struck by the sight of a crucifix, while travelling at Romsey, England, in "Christian Realism."

Rhetorical questioning, such as "Have you been lost?" ("The Christian Sense of Direction"), or "Are boys interested in trees?" ("Burning Bushes and Blackberries"), sets the congregation to thinking about personal experiences. In "Pilgrimage; Eden Lost and Emmaus Found," the initial questioning about what images the word "pilgrimage" conjures up is followed by a series of historical associations: from the historical *Mayflower* to the wars raging in the world, and from the various literatures on pilgrimage such as *The Canterbury Tales* to Malcolm X's autobiography, relating his pilgrimage to Mecca. The culmination of this device can be found in "The Christian Motive," which starts with eight rhetorical questions referring to historical examples showing the impact of Christian action throughout the centuries. Alternatively, this device can stimulate real questioning about one's faith.

Other less challenging beginnings, but as thoughtful, operate through contrast: contrast between two biblical texts written at different moments of the crucifixion-resurrection experience, in "The Tide Turned"; between administrative records and the records of the book of life, in "The Two

Census Books"; between Christianity and other religions, in "Death, Getaway." These contrasts are sometimes backed up by a string of powerful images, as in "Advent":

> If the commodious charabanc is the symbol of the Victorians, the compressed Austin-Seven is the symbol of today. The *Encyclopedia Britannica* has been ousted in favor of the *Reader's Digest*. The seven-course dinner retires in favor of the snack; the ponderous Family Bible is set aside for the Bedside Bible; the Old Testament is replaced by Moffat's version of the New. This desire for compression, this concentration on the essence, this Bovril for Beef, has advantages. If the Family Bible was used only as a paper-weight to hold the newspapers in place, then it is better to read the more manageable Moffat in an intelligible tongue. But this desire for compression and brevity has attendant dangers: the Sermon on the Mount is not the whole of the gospel; the New Testament is only understood on the background of the Old.

Thoughtfulness could also be inspired by a short avowal of the preacher's uncertainty, or humility, when he asks for the input of the congregation in examining a question, as in "The Holiness of Beauty," or "Faith and Fine Arts," where Davies tries to build bridges between God-lovers and art-lovers.

While other sermons employ the exegesis approach in their openings, the "Cross-examination" sermons form a series apart. Davies starts by summoning Mary, the mother, as if in a *séance*; in "Judas," he starts with the commonly accepted scathing verdict on Judas, then questions it reflectively, while, in "The Counselor: Joseph of Arimathea," he also criticizes the hagiographical reputation of the man on historical and sensible grounds. The portrait of the king, Herod, starts with a hymn, expressing judgment on human sinfulness. And three characters are featured in the setting of an imaginary newspaper report: Caiaphas, for whom Davies has no patience; Pontius Pilate; and the Soldier, the latter being interviewed as a token representative of the honest, no-nonsense, common man who, having witnessed the final words and breath of Jesus, paid him an unprejudiced tribute.

SERMONS' ENDINGS

Exhortation is the natural conclusion of the expounded text, leading towards Christian belief and its application, and consequently to a life of

Introduction I

dedication and service. Although we find several different methods in Davies's sermons, including some inconclusive endings requiring the congregation to ponder further, the most common, as found in the "Cross-examination" sermons, is a direct appeal to courage in confessing Christ and virtuous living. Christ's last words of care for the obedient Mary, he argues, assure us of his everlasting love. Judas's despair and broken heart is linked to ours by two small antithetical poems: one calls for a return to humility in despair, while the other reassures us that hope resides in Christ. The final message of "Caiaphas," "The King," "Pontius Pilate," and "Joseph of Arimathea" is to forsake hypocrisy, weak will, apathy, and fear, endorse the resolution of the Savior, and imitate the character of "The Soldier" in honestly confessing the holiness of Christ.

In other sermons, exhortation does not always appear in the form of a direct injunction. Some may finish with a question. "A Talk on Carols" asks whether the riches of traditional lore might not have been lost in the minimalist simplification of modernity. The Cloister, and the Hearth . . ." ends with the economic and social concerns that also appeared in "Protests, Profound, and Trivial" with the little girl's reported speech, "How far down dare I drink?" quoted later by Dr. Cain and serving as the title of this volume.

Five sermons end with quotations, giving the signature of authority: St. Paul's affirmation of having seen the light, in "Christian Certainties"; the repetition of the initial text by St. John, warning about the tribulations of the world and the final overcoming, at the end of "Christian Realism"; and the long quotation from *Pilgrim's Progress*, at the end of "The Two Census Books," promising a reward for whomever will force his or her way boldly into the Christian New Jerusalem.

Alternatively, Davies chooses to express his urgent message through hymns and poems: two poems conclude "Advent," one by Ray Palmer, perceiving the radiance of Christ, the other by trusting in the judgment of those who have actually seen and followed him. In the same spirit, the longest poem, by George MacDonald, ends "Glorifying the Cross." "It is the story," Davies says, "of a soul that shrank from the hard road but finally accepted it, and found happiness unspeakable."

Four sermons finish with a prayer. The longest at the end of "The Holiness of Beauty" is virtually a summary of the sermon. Others are short prayers of supplication. "The Christian Sense of Direction," and "Death, Getaway" are both marked by the anxiety caused by a world in turbulence:

How Far Down Dare I Drink?

> *O Thou, God of the living and not of the dead, grant us the assurance that in the grasp of Thy love, all is utterly safe; that our souls may commit unto Thee our life and what is far dearer than our life; that, throughout eternity, in Thy home, with Thee, to Thine own children never can harm befall, through Christ, the resurrection and the life. Amen*

Most sermons cling to the reassuring promise of Christ's forgiveness. In "Triple Victory," the prayer reaffirms Christ's victory over death, sin, and suffering, and expresses hope for personal resurrection and eternal life.

STRUCTURE

It has already been obvious that Davies's sermons were not in boring repetitive gray, with the same beginnings, and the same endings. That same variety applies to their structure.

Some sermons are based on the binary rhythm of contrast: "Advent," "The Two Census Books," "Burning Bushes and Blackberries," and "Eden Lost and Emmaus Found," with two illustrations derived from the realm of art: Spencer's *Last Supper*, and Rembrandt's *Emmaus*. "Advent" advocates a rich approach to Christianity including the Old Testament, rather than a reductionist view; "The Two Census Books" contrasts the stony way of strict administration to the rich and variegated way of life; "Burning Bushes and Blackberries" distinguishes the signs of material gain from the demands of service; "Christian Realism" deals with the external tribulations of life and the final overcoming; and "The Tide Turned" expounds on the Christian paradox applied to the psychological conversion of the soul.

Other sermons have a ternary structure: "Harvest Thanksgiving" expounds on beauty, truth, and conscience in that they form the essence of love. "Christian Realism" exposes three problems—sin, suffering, and death—and discusses their educational, political, and religious solutions. "Triple Victory" proclaims the victory of Christ over the three fears of physical death, the shrinking of the soul, and suffering. "Faith and Fine Art" has the Hegelian structure of thesis, antithesis, synthesis, proclaiming the importance of the alliance between art and religion for the revelation of beauty and truth. So has the second part of "The Cloister, and the Hearth . . ." After the initial expression of relief at reaching the day of graduation and congratulations to the community, Davies continues by asking the graduating class to obey God rather than persons, and debates,

Introduction I

among other concerns, the pros and cons of the feminist movement in Hegelian fashion.

"The Christian Sense of Direction" is a fine, multilayered version of the same three-tiered approach, each tier being subdivided in similar fashion: Luke's and John's texts address Christ's steadfastness of purpose. The sermon begins by reminding the members of the congregation of their own experiences of loss of direction—child, airman, yachtsman, and alpinist. Davies then moves to a higher level, the loss of purpose in life, and discusses three possible solutions: material things, conformity, or the ivory tower. Moving up to the Christian solutions, he rejects those three, and offers instead doing God's will, preaching the truth despite the fickleness of the crowd, having the courage of the lonely rider, who pursues his task steadfastly, despite feelings of dereliction. The prayer ends with an exhortation to follow Christ.

"Advent" stands alone for its structure; as a way of illustrating Hebrews 1:1, it is divided into seven points designed to link Christ to the prophets of the Old Testament.

Other sermons start from a text and run with it, almost by association: "Death, Gateway of Life Eternal," for instance. To explain the word "departure," used in 2 Timothy 4:6 to mean death, Davies takes a linguistic approach. The *Oxford English Dictionary* provides him with four striking uses of the word "departure" for the seaman, the ploughman, the traveler, and the philosopher to expand his congregation's vision of trust in Christ's promise in the resurrection. "The Christian Motive" starts with eight questions: most of the sermon consists in defining the two words "love" and "constraineth," and expanding on their relationship, which is also illustrated in two quoted poems. And "Glorifying in the Cross" starts with the scene of Christ in the garden of Gethsemane, pestered by his insecure disciples' competition for the best place in heaven, continues by sympathizing with the various ills and crosses the members of his congregation have been heirs to, and ends with an exhortation to hope and trust in the words of the Lord.

RHETORICAL DEVICES

In *Like Angels from a Cloud*,[2] Davies expressed his admiration for the "metaphysical" preachers:

---

2. Horton Davies, *Like Angels from a Cloud: The English Metaphysical Preachers 1588–1645* (San Marino, California: Huntington Library, 1986), p. 483.

> What a grey and color-blind universe would be presented to our eyes if sermons lacked all ornament, and these poet preachers left us entirely devoid of images and illustrations! To use Fuller's image, we should be living in churches with ample and reasonable pillars, but inside walls without windows.

"Plain" and biblical though they may be, Davies's sermons are not dull, but varied in their vocabulary, structure, beginnings, and endings.

As we have partly seen, he also used rhetoric for a purpose, in questions, parallelism, oppositions, enumerations, and repetitions, separately or in conjunction, as in Baptist preaching. We have already quoted the beginning of "Advent." Let us quote the string of rhetorical questions in "The Christian Motive":

> What is the motive of Christian service? What built our medieval cathedrals with their graceful spires or climbing towers, with their miraculous rainbowed windows, their embossed roofs and fan-tracery? What drove Bach to write his *St. John's Passion,* and Handel to compose his *Messiah*? What sent Livingstone into the dark and treacherous heart of an unknown continent? What drove Elizabeth Fry to the vermin-infested prisons of England day after day? What sent Ignatius, an octogenarian, manfully to face the lions in the Roman arena? What makes hundreds of thousands of believers the world over to worship, each Sunday, and to their knees each night? What is the power that enables men and women to face suffering, bereavement and catastrophe unshaken and still confident? What is the motive of all sacrifice and unselfishness?

Or the mixture of rhetorical questioning and exclamation marks to show Davies's emotions in "The Christian Sense of Direction":

> The crowd! How could we go with the crowd that cried: "Hosanna in the Highest!" [Matthew 21:9] when they thought he was the leader of a New Deal, and: "Crucify Him!" [see Matthew 27:22–23] when they preferred a Robin Hood like Barabbas ? . . . The changeling crowd!

In contrast, one could quote the series of short sentences of "Triple Victory" expressing the shortness of breath due to the pangs of the relieved heart:

> He had crossed the frontier of death and he had come home. Their Christ, God the son, was home from the World-War. Now they knew they could shout: "O death, where thy sting / O grave, where

is thy Victory?" [see I Corinthians 15:55]. No need for them to speak of death, as the country from whose [boundary] no traveler returns. "He showed himself alive after his Passion." The Victim of the Cross was the Victor. The Sacrifice of the Cross was not wasted. Nothing good is wasted in the universe over which God reigns. The cross is the victorious Cross. Christ returns alive after crossing the frontier of death. God wins; if we are on God's side, we win.

At other times Davies uses humor, and his Oxford-learnt wit appears in pithy sentences. "The Christian Motive" attacks the idea of Christianity as an insurance policy, "with a heavenly grandfather with a benign smile and a pocketful of comforts." Another time, he satirizes a cowardly clergyman who, facing an empty collection plate after a daring sermon which must have offended some parishioners, turned towards his acolyte and said, "Next week, back to the generalities."

The longest and most amusing satirical passage occurs in "Faith and Fine Art" about traditional church architecture:

> The Protestant Meeting-house in the Puritan tradition says, "The God we worship finds color dangerous. He prefers the black and white of carefully etched lives to the color and sprawl of individuality." The Methodist Church, with its curdled milk stained-glass windows, says, "My haloed Jesus was a safe, warm, sentimental Savior; irrelevant for the daily world of crises, but fine for the family on Sundays." The Presbyterian Church, with its deliberate absence of the historic symbols of Christianity, says through its cubes, diamonds, squares, triangles, circles, and fleurs-de-lys, "I believe in geometry." The plain Jewish Synagogue, as free of symbolism, with the exception of the Star of David, as the Presbyterian, or the Baptist Church, says, "Our God is to be served in the Community; beauty is a distraction." The Roman Catholic Church says, "We will use art for the purposes of religious propaganda, to remind you, by our images of Christ, the Virgin, and the saints, of your duty through these examples." And as we listen, we think, "How very conventional these statues are; we've seen them repeated in plastic in a supermarket a thousand times."

Here Davies pounds his congregation with enumerations of the religious artists he admires: Epstein, Rouault, Chagall, the icons of the Eastern Orthodox churches, Botticelli, Hans Memling, Michelangelo and Rembrandt, in that order; to which one can add Piper, and Sutherland, from

"The Holiness of Beauty," and Spencer, from "Pilgrimage: Eden Lost and Emmaus Found."

Davies does not usually indulge in mordant satire. Most of the time, his is the compassionate style, with some lyrical passages, and vivid portraits, as in the "Cross-Examination."

For a lyrical passage one might turn to "Christian Certainties in an Uncertain World," with its prolonged metaphor on light and the lighthouse:

> The sea rages, darkness comes over the land, but the lighthouse stands, and steadily the light is transmitted for the warning and the comfort of the sea's wayfarers. It stands immovable on the rock, solid in the flux and change of the elements. This is a parable of the Revelation of God in the uncertain world of the atomic Age. I would remind you this evening of the radiant certainties that flash forth from God's Revelation, making his Word a lamp unto your feet.

OTHER TECHNIQUES; THE PORTRAIT.

This introduction cannot be exhaustive. As in the previous introductions to *Believing* and to *Preaching to a World in Crisis*, we could have spoken of the church historians and saints that Horton Davies admired. One could have spoken of his ecumenism and the interest in other religions that he touched on in his course on religion and literature. We could have quoted passages where he expresses his admiration for Lincoln, Roosevelt, and Kennedy.

But here we want to leave room for the art of the portrait: physical, behavioral, and psychological, as seen in the Jewish and Roman characters of the "Cross-Examination" series, which shows that Davies himself had integrated the techniques of the writers he admired most and paid homage to, in "The Value of Modern Fiction for Preachers": vivification of vocabulary, imagination, and empathy, as in the works of James Baldwin, Frederick Buechner, William Golding, Graham Greene, John Updike, and Elie Wiesel, to name only a few. David Cain, in his introduction, aptly quotes at length *A Church Historian's Odyssey*. I will only quote here a few words: "I tried to make their presence as vivid as possible . . . [These sermons were] an illustration of the vividness of the narrative, the psychological relevance, and the sympathy required of all preachers to gain and to hold the attention of a congregation."³

In "Advent," Davies had already shown some talent at creating a small theatrical scene among the prophets he had summoned from *The King comes to Zion*, a Russian icon. Even more telling was the portrait of Moses and his dog in "Burning Bushes and Blackberries." The narrative sets the scene of shepherd (Moses), dog, and sheep looking for greener pastures, and of Moses's encounter with God at the burning bush. The point of view is omniscient. We enter the minds of two leaders: that of Moses, concerned for his people, but also the dog's, mindful of his sheep, and dreaming of his bone.

It is this kind of artful empathy that we find in the "Cross-Examination" series. In "The Mother," Davies proceeds from the physical description of the bereaved Mary, to the evocation of the turmoil of her soul in three sections: a recollection of the distant past with the happy days of Jesus's childhood; the parental concerns and misunderstandings at his coming of age in the synagogue; the difficult acceptance of and wonder at the mystery of the adult Jesus. Her only uttered words ring like a dirge: "O God, the waste, the waste of it!" or "O God, the folly, the folly of it!" The conclusion, coming after her acceptance of her son's life and ministry, is an exhortation to a life of obedience and faith.

"Judas" softens the usual demonizing of the character, by trying to guess why he had been chosen by Jesus, and why he betrayed him. The point of view at first is external, the psychological evaluation mostly behavioral; then comes Davies's moral judgment on why Judas became a traitor to Jesus: a mixture of greed and resentment at Christ's "shafts of truth" about greed, and political ambition. Then the point of view becomes internal, as we are led into the mind of Judas to try to recreate the underlying emotional basis of his political beliefs within the Judean historical context. The transactions with the priests are recorded in dialogue form. Davies quotes another bemused writer, Masefield, for whom Judas was also a puzzle. After two short poems comes the warning: the face you see may be your own. Beware and repent!

Davies has no sympathy for Caiaphas, the archpriest, traitor to a fellow Jew. The scene is set with an imaginary newspaper headline: "Archbishop demands death penalty for preaching."

3. Horton Davies, *A Church Historian's Odyssey: A Memoir* (Allison Park, Pennsylvania: Pickwick Publications, 1993), pp. 20–21.

How Far Down Dare I Drink?

Yet again an explanation is sought, in the difference of temperaments and social backgrounds between Caiaphas and Jesus. The archpriest of the Sadducees is portrayed through association, as being as cold and rigid as the priest who passed the injured man on the way to Jericho. He is labeled as a snob, trembling in fear for a career made through connections. He is contrasted with the carpenter's son, a self-made rabbi, warm and generous, a man of principle who made a distinction between room for commerce and a space for prayer and worship. Animal imagery derived from the Fabliaux tradition delineates the moral and behavioral portrait of Caiaphas, which is completed in "Pontius Pilate": a viper, hooded, and coiled to strike, who, with great intelligence, will pressure the new appointed ruler to sacrifice Jesus for the sake of the union of church and state, a self-serving decision taken under the strain of fear and panic that does not, however, cloud his cunning. Rhetoric emphasizes with the repeated phrase: "Caiaphas was a Sadducee." Young Davies, however, tries to understand the man under pressure, his fears for his job, the approaching time of the Passover and of the Sabbath during the Jewish unrest against the Roman colonist, and the opportune temptation offered by Judas, which led him to break the Jewish law by a rushed trial at night, and send an innocent to the cross. It ends with this severe condemnation: "And notice this: this insincere priest exploited the very sincerity of the prisoner. With this unsavory incident, I close the curtain over a whited sepulcher, a character whose deeds reek of the charnel-house, and smell foul after the winds of twenty centuries have swept across the earth."

Yet the final word is one of hope for all dire sinners, in Jesus's words of forgiveness.

"The King" starts with an indictment of the human race in two short verses. Medieval lore also serves to characterize Herod the Tetrarch by comparing him to Reynard the Fox. Davies recalls his Shakespearian sensitivity for a haunted man who, for trivial reasons, had killed a prophet whom he loved and admired. He portrays him as a sort of Macbeth, "clever, undoubtedly, and cultured, and interested in religion." Davies imagines his mixture of joy and fear at seeing this new resurrected John the Baptist in Jesus, and yet deeply troubled by what might be a Banquo-like return of the dead. With the help of the narrative of the dance of Salome, Davies transforms Herod into an overgrown adolescent who shuns his responsibilities, and saves face by making a travesty of a situation he cannot handle, and passing

Introduction I

the buck to Pilate. The sermon ends on an emotional appeal to seriousness, warmth of heart, and compassion:

> I would give everything in the world to bring a smile to that tortured sad face, to see it light up as the prodigal came home, and to hear the bells of heaven chiming as if they would break with sheer joy. Wouldn't you?

In "Pontius Pilate" that character, no longer a beast, reaches the stature of a man, fresh in his new job, and therefore of interest to the "newspapers" of the day. As a self-appointed legal correspondent, Davies uses a brief, journalistic style and a variety of voices for different interviewees. The Wallington congregation would be amused at Pilate's wife being called "Lady Claudia." Davies uses history to the full as a basis for his creation: two major reports are presented to delineate the historical circumstances of Pilate's uncourageous decision: a soldier's and a priest's, who tell of Pilate's first rash actions, and the Jews' seething revolt. Davies seems to have compassion for Pilate, pressured by Caiaphas's political acumen and the historical situation. Pilate had already confronted the Jewish mob; he wanted law and order. Caiaphas offers a truce thanks to a sacrifice, as a sort of passing beneficial union of church and state, which was dear to the Romans whose emperor was adored as a god. Nor did the Romans hesitate at encouraging the self-sacrifice, voluntary or not, of rebels or deviants cumbersome to the state. So where was the difficulty in sacrificing Jesus? Davies does not portray Pilate as a fool: he asks Caiaphas to repeat publicly his grounds for accusation, but, unfortunately, does not pursue himself the interrogation; during his personal interview with Jesus, he cannot see the truth. Davies has sympathy for this newcomer, distracted by the novelty of a job full of snares, and having already faced twice a mob on the rise. No doubt some modern examples must have been on Davies's mind, but he does not tell.

Davies simply uses his mirror-holding technique, and asks why such a simple story should have carried so much weight over the centuries; he argues that the obvious answer is that Jesus's self-sacrifice was not accidental, but planned by God for the redemption of humanity.

In "The city-counselor, Joseph of Arimathea," Davies keeps his distance from the hagiographical Glastonbury legend, with what he imagines must have been the truth of the character. He depicts the administrator as a mere sensitive man rather than a saint, on grounds of historical evidence gathered from the four gospels, and from common sense. Once more Davies asks his congregation to stand in the shoes of his character, and enter his mindset by means of several snippets of reported speech. His choice of vocabulary demonstrates his prudence; "wait," "seemed," "if you're a sensible man, you'll lie low," "stay at home," "Lie low, Joseph!" (repeated three times) "I have my position to think of," etc . . . Then, by evocation, Davies continues to illuminate the thoughts that eventually spurred him to action.

The exhortation is a call for commitment, in the name of Christ, despite the fear of ridicule and criticism.

In "The Soldier," the centurion is respectfully depicted as the Roman upright man, respectful of authority, but devoid of prejudices, a man of few words, who will tell the truth as he sees it. To assess the reliability of his witness, Davies, as he had done with Herod, uses the convergence of three stories: that of the centurion of Capernaum, coming to plead with Jesus to heal his servant; of Cornelius who converted; and of Julius, who entertained a cordial relationship with Paul. The case is built by association: centurions are to be trusted. Davies, however, has to recreate a true-to-life character: this he does by reminding the congregation of the centurion's gory profession as soldier, and as chief executioner. But the centurion's character as an honest man remains intact. The enumeration of the last utterances of the agonizing Jesus, sentence by sentence, and paragraph by paragraph, builds up the case, as in a law court, and leaves no doubt in the mind of that wondering, simple, honest man. His words of tribute are uttered, almost despite himself as a man who is used to obey orders, in the face of Jesus's meek and kind behavior.

Davies, having addressed the doubts of faltering faith, urges his congregation to become evangelists of Christ.

In all his sermons, Davies argues that "we are saved by hope" given to us by the overcoming on the cross. Modern thinkers, like the prophets, rightly despair of the spiritual progress of human beings. Christian hope looks back to the resurrections of the past (the Reformation, Christian victory over the Saracens, revivals in the church, and the conversion of St. Francis) to find hope for the future. Like Wordsworth, Davies praises wise old men whose hearts are not troubled. Longing for long-term hope, hope for eternity that liberates by asserting the sacredness of human beings, he calls for evangelists of a hope based on faith in Christ the healer, love incarnate, obedient to the Father. The preacher's task, as Davies reminds us, is to appeal to the reverence of life eternal.

Introduction II
How Far Down Dare I Drink?
Promises Greater than Dreams

David Cain

From a catch of some sixty-four sermons, with a few others coming along, and with some duplications with modest variations, making the count also variable, I have selected the sermons which follow, not on the basis of content or of chronology (which is often not known), but on the basis of what I take to be quality and interest. Volume I of Horton Davies's sermons, *Believing*,[1] was organized content-wise in relation to traditional church creeds. A kind of chronology appropriately and effectively ordered volume II, *Preaching to a World in Crisis*,[2] from World War II in England, to South Africa, to America. That is the way I would have gone, following Horton Davies, *A Church Historian's Odyssey: A Memoir*,[3] had it not already been done. For chronology in Horton Davies's odyssey is significant. So I selected, sometimes almost arbitrarily, the sermons. Then I read those I had chosen to see if some configurations suggested themselves. The result is the shape of this book in three sections: "Responses to Gospel,"

---

1. Horton Davies, *Believing: Sermons by Horton Davies*, eds. John Booty and Marie-Hélène Davies (Eugene, Oregon: Wipf and Stock Publishers, 2007).

2. Horton Davies, *Preaching to a World in Crisis: Sermons by Horton Davies*, eds. Marie-Hélène Davies and Henry Bowden (Eugene, Oregon: Wipf and Stock Publishers, 2009).

3. Horton Davies, *A Church Historian's Odyssey*.

"Cross-Examination," and "Faith and Art" (but elsewhere the aesthetic is never far away).

Just next to Christian faith in the life and thought of Horton Davies is the aesthetic[4]—literature,[5] music, architecture (notice the architectural attentiveness in these sermons[6]), art—above all art. The late years of his life most appropriately saw an explosion of color, of paintings of cathedrals, of flowers, plants, of whimsy: a distinctive style; a remarkable technique chiefly in acrylics and water colors.

Perhaps the best introduction to this third volume of sermons of Horton Davies is his own work: *A Church Historian's Odyssey: A Memoir*. Read this work as a personal accompaniment to the sermons, but also for its surprise and adventure, and for the fascinating and illustrious cast of characters we meet along the way.[7] This word "Odyssey" is worth lingering over—literarily (Homer), historically, autobiographically, and etymologically (Odysseus's decade of wandering). Though etymology is not involved, no harm is done in allowing "odyssey" to suggest "odd."

Early on, in characterizing his father, David Marlais Davies, a Congregational minister, Horton Davies provides reflexively an effective portrait of himself as preacher:

> I, of course, heard him preach many times in English[8] and what I remember as outstanding was his sonorous and mellifluous voice

---

4. Horton Davies was a great admirer of Georges Rouault (1871–1958) of whom he writes, "Rouault was . . . an impressive evangelist in esthetics"—Horton Davies, "Rouault Reconsidered as a Christian Painter," *The American Benedictine Review*, vol. 44, no. 4 (December, 1993), p. 382. So was Horton Davies.

5. "English literature was my first love . . ."—Horton Davies, *A Mirror of the Ministry in Modern Novels* (New York: Oxford University Press, 1959), p. ix. This first love is everywhere evidenced in Horton Davies's sermons.

6. See below pp. 55, 180–182.

7. Too bad there is no "Index of Names." (I went some way toward producing one, but the project began to seem unwieldy.) One of the treats of *Odyssey* is the persons we meet on most every page. This remarkably diverse band dramatizes Horton Davies's gregariousness. He liked people—all kinds.

8. Of course he preached also in Welsh. One of the most vivid and, in many ways, moving moments of my life was in Llanberis, Wales, on Sunday, 29 September, 1963, Nant Padarn Congregational Chapel. I understood not a word. Suddenly I understood. The pastor had apparently spotted me, a foreigner. How he knew I spoke English I do

that could declaim with indignation and whisper in compassion, his memorable illustrations, and his psychological analyses, all of which held the attention of his congregations enthralled.⁹

Davies does not ask about or argue for the truth of the Christian faith. He begins there. I recall a conversation from years ago with Langdon Gilkey, and an image with which we played: getting to the top of *Festung Hohensalzburg*.¹⁰ How do you get there? Well, there is a cog railway. Or you can walk. Once there, you can look down on Salzburg, or "out the back" to the plane and the Alps in the distance.¹¹ Davies does not ask how one

---

not know. He summarized the sermon in English—for me. I found that overwhelmingly touching, and much of the touch was the magic and mystery of language.

I was in fact on a kind of pilgrimage—to Horton Davies's birthplace in Cwmavon, Glamorganshire, Wales, which I found on Tuesday, 1 October, 1963. I walked in off-and-on rain the two or three miles from Port Talbot, east of Swansea, through Aberavon (Aber: "the place where a river discharges into the sea or into another river," Afon—"a river"—*Ward Lock's Red Guide: South Wales* [London: Ward, Lock & Co., Limited, London, 1963], p. 10) to Cwmavon (valley river). There I was directed to a Mr. D. T. Eaton, the village historian, at 2 Tabernacle Terrace. He knew of Horton Davies's father coming to Cwmavon in 1914 as minister of Eglwys Seion (Zion Church), of the birth of Daniel Timothy Horton Davies in 1916, 10 March, and of the family's move to Manchester in 1919. (I include this information for the possible interest of some readers.) Mr. Eaton told me that about three years ago (c. 1960), D. Marlais Davies had returned to Cwmavon with his two sons, Horton, being the oldest, and Dorian. They had sat together in the room in which I now sat and had had a "town meeting" that evening, in which Horton and then his father spoke. Mr. Eaton recalled this as a "most enjoyable evening." Mr. Eaton then guided me on an "expedition" to 15 Victoria Terrace ("Fairhill") where Horton Davies had been born. Next we called upon 8 Victoria Terrrace, the residence of Mrs. R. D. Daniel or Katie Bowen, who had taken care of blue-eyed, curly-haired Horton, who had known her as "Katie" and who "always liked to be dirty." I received a letter from Mr. D. T. Eaton dated 16 October, 1963, post marked "Port Talbot." It reads in part: "You succeeded in finding the home of Dr. Horton Davies. Brgnteg [I'm not sure I am reading the handwriting accurately], 23 Victoria Terrace [nor can I account for the discrepancies], and you also spoke to the lady that nursed him, Mrs. R. D. Daniel, 8 Victoria Terrace. I should imagine that Dr. Horton Davies was about 3 years old when his family left for Manchester in 1919."

9. Davies, *A Church Historian's Odyssey*, p. 3.

10. See Langdon Gilkey, *Naming the Whirlwind: The Renewal of God-Language* (Indianapolis: The Bobbs-Merrill Company, 1969), pp. 199–200, n. 9.

11. I cannot resist recalling a splendid, enchanted experience. This was Friday, 27 December, 1963, Salzburg. After a dismal day of rain and dark and gloom, I climbed up (the railway was not running) to the *Festung* only to see an unexpected glow. Hurrying on up to the top, I saw out of "back" side around the *Festung*, across a vast plane, or so I thought, the red setting sun cutting through the heavy grey-black clouds and bleeding over and backlighting brilliantly the jagged teeth of the Alps. I had not known the Alps

gets there. He climbs up (or is lifted[12]). The challenge is in looking around, looking down, looking out from the perspective of the gospel. What does one see? We shall see what we shall see. This is where Horton Davies abides and roams. And the vindication of the Christian faith, even the validation, is in the light shed on the motley world from one's risked vantage point. Validation is not *to the gospel* but *from the gospel*. What Davies sees is real suffering, real death, real defeat—and real victory, all the more glorious because of the reality of that over which the victory has been won.

In a sermon called "Worship and the Renewal of the Church 5,[13] Preaching Contemporizing Christ," Davies gives us a sermon on sermons (there is more than one such sermon on sermons: the abiding concern with preaching). I quote at length from the beginning:

> As we ask ourselves what preaching really is, we may be helped to understand it from three very different definitions. Here is one from Dean Inge of St. Paul's Cathedral,[14] and the gloomy dean naturally first thought of the difficulty, impossibility of try-

---

were there. I wrote at the time: "A tremendously long and difficult climb ... Turning left and walking down steps, I emerged onto an open balcony, overlooking the back door of Salzburg to the south and to the west; and the sight in the west was perhaps the most remarkable single sight my eyes have yet beheld in nature. The all-grey-and-black of all in the tangible world draped in a mystery of white, moving mist broke away from the immediate glory of a brilliant blaze, cutting through the stubborn strata of low clouds in the west and burning the ragged, monstrous outline of the secret Alps down into the valley."

12. This is of pressing importance. God and persons: who is searching for whom? Horton Davies refers to Francis Thompson's "The Hound of Heaven"—God's pursuit of us (see *Mirror of the Ministry*, p. 105, and Horton Davies, *Catching the Conscience: Essays in Religion and Literature* (Cambridge, Massachusetts: Cowley Publications, 1984), p. 95). C. S. Lewis writes, "The odd thing was that before God closed in on me, I was in fact offered what now appears a moment of wholly free choice. In a sense, I was going up Headington Hill on the top of a bus." And then: "You must picture me alone in that room in Magdalen, night after night, feeling, whenever my mind lifted even for a second from my work, the steady, unrelenting approach of Him [we are very close to "The Hound of Heaven"] whom I so earnestly desired not to meet." Lewis describes himself as "perhaps, that night, the most dejected and reluctant convert in all England"—C. S. Lewis, *Surprised by Joy: The Shape of My Early Life* (New York: Harcourt, Brace & World, Inc., 1955), pp. 224, 228-229. Or Abraham Joshua Heschel appropriately titles a book on the Hebrew Bible, *God in Search of Man*.

13. Obviously this is part of a series. I have located one other unnumbered "Worship and the Renewal of the Church" sermon ("Prayer") but not the others.

14. William Ralph Inge (1860-1954) was an Anglican priest, professor of divinity at Cambridge, prolific author, and dean of St. Paul's Cathedral (1911-1934), hence "Dean Inge."

ing to educate individuals aged from eight to eighty, with a variety of temperaments and of different educational backgrounds and experience in one twenty-minute lesson a Sunday. So he wrote: "Preaching is like trying to fill rows of narrow necked vessels by throwing buckets of water over them." Obviously a lot of water would be spilled, but one hoped that a few drops would percolate down the necks!

Now turn to another definition by the great American preacher Phillips Brooks of Boston.[15] He was thinking of how Christianity is not only taught, but it is caught. It is doctrine conveyed in a Christ-imitating spirit. So his famous definition reads: "Preaching is truth conveyed through personality."

Next we turn to a distinguished layman and Cambridge historian, Bernard Lord Manning.[16] He wrote: "It is a manifestation of the Incarnate Word, from the Written Word by the Spoken Word; it is a most solemn act of worship, in which the thing given—the gospel of the Son of God—overshadows and even transfigures the preacher by whom it is declared." That, I think, is a very profound definition. It suggests that Christ the Word made flesh is the gospel, that the Scriptures are the written record of his coming, and that the Spoken Word of the preacher contemporizes Christ, makes him our present savior and example by the power of the Holy Spirit. One could perhaps make a slight addition. That the end of preaching is that Christ's Word should take flesh in us, so that we become God's witnesses in action.

My fourth definition [a "bonus" definition: we were promised three] comes from a distinguished Presbyterian minister and university professor at Cambridge, Herbert H. Farmer.[17] It is brief, but very much to the point. He calls the preacher simply The Servant of the Word. He has no other authority than to proclaim God's message, not his own opinions. In other words if the preacher is not under the authority of the Word of God he is overreaching himself and has become overbearing. His task is to say, as John the Baptist did of our Lord: I must decrease and he must increase" [John 3:30]. The converse is also unfortunately true: "The more I increase, the more Christ must decrease."

---

15. Phillips Brooks (1835–1893) was an Episcopal priest, author, and Bishop of Massachusetts, 1891–1893.

16. Bernard Lord Manning (1892–1941) was an author who taught medieval history at Cambridge University.

17. Herbert Henry Farmer (1892–1981) was a Presbyterian minister, Cambridge Professor of Systematic Theology and Apologetics, and an author of important works such as *The Servant of the Word* (1941).

How Far Down Dare I Drink?

Davies proceeds to distinguish a sermon from an essay, a lecture, or a political speech and concludes:

> A sermon, then, is a type of discourse that tries to provide a combination of religious instruction and exhortation. It aims at light and heat. It is revelation and transformation, appealing to both the mind and the will through the imagination.

Imagination: read on.

Then Davies asks, "Since I have called preaching "contemporizing Christ," how can I apply this to our desperate twentieth century needs [needs no less desperate in the twenty-first century]? Let me try to do so in five major ways . . ." These five needs-ways are futility, insignificance, insecurity, fear, and Christ-shaped emptiness. We cannot but think here of Augustine's famous restless heart:

> Yet man, this part of your creation, wishes to praise you. You arouse him to take joy in praising you, for you have made us for yourself, and our heart is restless until it rests in you.[18]

We must not miss the positive regard for and recurring commendation of imagination, wedded to the aesthetic.[19] Davies was devoted to a line from Graham Greene's *The Power and the Glory*, about which he wrote:[20] "hate is 'a failure of the imagination.'"[21] In the work of Horton Davies, the primacy of the imagination means: no hate. Indeed—and one can see this in his writing and in his person—a kind, gentle, gracious, affirming personality predominated.

Davies exuded an unaffected, elegant charm, a crisp, fresh presence. Being in his presence was a pleasure, and one *could* be in his presence. He was here and not somewhere else. He was present in wit, earnestness, word-play, kindness, and caring. He was intellectually astute fun. A twinkle was in his eye.

Horton Davies, lover of words and of the Word. He plays on words: "Cross-Examination," an examination *across*, back-and-forth, and an examination of a Cross and by a Cross examining all, questioning all, putting all to the test. Another example: wonder. More than one sermon ends

---

18. Saint Augustine of Hippo, *The Confessions of St. Augustine*, trans. John K. Ryan (Garden City, New York: Doubleday & Company, Inc., 1960), p. 43 (Book 1, Chapter 1).

19. See esp. "The Value of Modern Fiction for Preachers," pp. 170–179 below.

20. *Catching the Conscience*, pp. 95–107.

21. *Catching the Conscience*, p. 104. See p. 2. See also *A Mirror of the Ministry*, p. 107.

Introduction II

with "I wonder." That is, I question. I wonder. That is, I marvel. For Horton Davies, the latter wonder surrounded and subsumed if not subdued the former. I wonder. How far down dare I drink?

Back to *A Church Historian's Odyssey*. In chapter 2, "Minister of a South London Church" (Wallington and Carshalton in Surrey where he was for three and a half years, 1942–1946), Davies refers to his series sermons—"Christian Convictions" (six sermons), "Jesus, Monarch of Men" (eleven sermons[22]), "Christ and Human Need" (four sermons), "The Divinity of Our Lord" (three sermons), "Christianity" (three sermons), "The Challenge of the Sects" (sermon count unclear, perhaps ten[23]). Then there is "Cross-Examination." Since this series of seven sermons is included as the second section in the present volume, I quote at length what Davies writes about it:

> I preached a series of sermons on the Crucifixion as an event and illustrated its meaning then and now by the responses to it. The title, which was advertised boldly outside the church for passersby to see clearly, was CROSS-EXAMINATION, and several different witnesses were considered. I tried to make their presence as vivid as possible. I can give as an example my treatment of the first witness, Mary, the mother of Jesus, recorded by the gospel of John 19:25, as follows: "Standing by the cross of Jesus, his mother . . ." The sermon began:[24] . . .
>
> Using my imagination, I assumed that the first reaction was the sense of sheer futility of the Cross, and the second the sheer folly of it and its appalling waste consequent on Christ's verbal attacks on the Scribes and Pharisees of Jerusalem. Then came the third reaction, very late. Perhaps Jesus was right. His accusers were mistaken: he was never a blasphemer. As for the superscription on the Cross that he claimed to be king of the Jews, this too was mistaken for he had always refused to be a popular political leader. Then I continued:[25] . . .
>
> And the meaning for modern Maries and Josephs struck by tragedies is to learn the obedience of faith, for in the words of a

---

22. Five sermons in this series are included in *Preaching to a World in Crisis*, pp. 183–207.

23. This estimate is based on the chapters in the book (twelve including an introduction and conclusion), Horton Davies, *Christian Deviations* (London: Student Christian Movement Press, 1954), also published as *The Challenge of the Sects* (Philadelphia: The Westminster Press, 1961).

24. See pp. 129–162 below.

25. See p. 132 below.

modern theologian, "The Incarnation began when Mary said, 'Into Thy hands I commend my body,' and ended when Jesus said, 'Into thy hands I commend my spirit.'" I ended with the following words:

> Those who keep tryst with God through the dark night of trial shall see the clouds of darkness hurrying before the golden chariots of Easter dawn. Nothing can separate us from the love of God in Christ Jesus our Lord [see Romans 8]. Nothing.[26]

This example of a greatly condensed and summarized sermon is merely an illustration of the vividness of narrative, the psychological relevance, and the sympathy required of all preachers to gain and to hold the attention of a congregation.

A similar technique was employed in the cross-examination of Judas Iscariot, Caiaphas, King Herod the fox, Pontius Pilate, Joseph of Arimathea the City Counselor, and the Soldier, totally seven witnesses in all, and others, such as Peter, could have been added to the number for Mark 14:50 records "all the disciples forsook him and fled."[27]

Evidenced here is the literary and dramatic sensitivity and sensibility which are indispensable in Davies's sermons. Recurring themes in these sermons are "Christian realism": death is death; God's promises persist and prevail; imagination is an agent of life; theodicy.

We encounter a wonderful range of awareness and reference—theologically, historically, literarily, artistically, and poetically. Reading Davies's sermons offers adventure because we never know what—or who—is coming next. The breadth and range and interests are so great that we may find ourselves in any century, any culture, and any world. Davies steps up to the pulpit "off the street," as it were. There is immediacy, directness in his preaching, a matter-of-factness, sincerity, quiet passion, patient urgency, and zest. He likes to juxtapose two biblical texts—aligned, allied, contrasting, mutually and variously engaging (see, for example, "The Tide Turned: Transfiguration—Mount of Triumph, Mount of Defeat" and "The Two Census Books: Income Tax, Outcome Tax"). Then he inserts his own observations on connections and disconnections often with the help of great writers, artists, and others. The recurring reference to the prophets of the Hebrew Bible in relation to Christ is important (see, for example, "Advent: Fulfillment and Finality").

---

26. See p. 132 below.
27. *A Church Historian's Odyssey*, p. 162.

Rich phrases fortify the sermons. Watch for them: "that crimson love," "costly compassion," "the ape warring with the angel in each of us,"[28] "a wound in the heart of God from the beginning of time," "one more generation of the prisoners of death," "uncontrollable skidding in the automobile of life," "[e]ach one for himself as the elephant said when he danced among the chickens,"[29] "the rickety bridge of faith."

The three-part structure of this volume is not deliberately trinitarian; yet, as it turns out, the first section seems to relate to God the Father (though perichoresis is ever with us); certainly section two relates to God the Son; and section three implicates effectively the Spirit. I think Davies would agree.

"Loving God, Loving Art" works both ways. The love of God is God's love (subjective genitive). The love of God is also love for God (objective genitive). The love of art is the love which art manifests (subjective genitive) as well as our love for art (objective genitive). Davies knew and bore witness to the recognition and conviction that here was no "either / or" but a joyous "both / and." As Davies insists in "Faith and Fine Art: Loving God, Loving Art":

---

28. I have sought to resist this reference but have obviously failed: the epigraph of Søren Kierkegaard's pseudonymous *Stages on Life's Way* ("Compiled, Forwarded to the Press, and Published by Hilarius Bookbinder") is Lichtenberg's (Georg Christoph Lichtenberg [1742–1799]) "*Solche Werke sind Spiegel: wenn ein Affe hinein guckt, kann kein Apostel heraus sehen*" —"Such works are mirrors: when an ape looks in, no apostle can look out"—Søren Kierkegaard, *Stages on Life's Way: Studies by Various Persons*, ed. and trans Howard V. Hong and Edna H. Hong, (Princeton: Princeton University Press, 1988), p. 8, Kierkegaard's Writings XI. An apostle is not angel, but an analogy obtains. And how near are we to Dmitri Karamazov? "Yes, man is broad, too broad, indeed. I'd have him narrower"—Fyodor Dostoevsky, *The Brothers Karamazov*, trans. Constance Garnett, rev. Avrahm Yarmolinsky (New York: The Heritage Press, 1949), pp. 79–80. This odd Christian God takes risks. Kenneth Cragg, Anglican priest, Islamicist deeply invested in Christian-Muslim relations (1913–2012), once referred to the Christian God as "the God who has gone out on a limb." Scarry. A close reading of Davies's sermons indicates this recognition.

29. I am reminded of Johannes Climacus' reference: ". . . where the ethical becomes as shy as a sparrow in a dance of cranes," Søren Kierkegaard, *Concluding Unscientific Postscript to* Philosophical Fragments, I, ed. and trans. Howard V. Hong and Edna H. Hong (Princeton: Princeton University Press, 1992), p. 142. But this image is not original with Climacus—or Kierkegaard. The Hongs provide the following note: "A Danish expression used by Jens Christian Hostrup as the title of the student comedy *En Spurv i Tranedands* (Copenhagen: 1846)," Søren Kierkegaard, *Concluding Unscientific Postscript to* Philosophical Fragments, II, ed. and trans. Howard V. Hong and Edna H. Hong (Princeton: Princeton University Press, 1992), p. 218, n. 177.

> The true life of religion is for the whole personality, for body as well as soul, for feelings as well as will, for the imagination as well as the intellect. This means that we must be open to all the creativity of the supreme artist who paints sunsets and roses, who stripes the tigers and zebras, and forms the poignant loveliness of human beauty, too.[30]

A Church Historian's Odyssey offers what may be surprises—from seminary budgets and faculty salaries to the geology of the Grand Canyon. But no surprise is the recurring interest and investment in preaching[31] and church architecture.[32] It is as if these are partners, not of Davies's passion alone—and passion it was—but of one another. Davies had a holistic sense of the time of the word and the space into which the word resonated and might be received.

The sermons of Horton Davies are ever and always, first and last, responses to gospel, and this means, in his understanding of gospel, responses to promise. As noted earlier, a cardinal word in these sermons is "imagination." Perhaps imagination is second only to "promises." An old hymn is "Standing on the Promises":

> Standing on the promises of Christ, my king,
> Through eternal ages let His praises ring,
> Glory in the highest, I will shout and sing,
> Standing on the promises of God.
>
> Standing, standing,
> Standing on the promises of God my Savior;
> Standing, standing,
> I'm standing on the promises of God.[33]

As these sermons attest, here Horton Davies stood. And this takes imagination.

A sermon or an address in this volume, "The Cloister, and the Hearth, and the Community,"[34] concludes with a stirring story from South Africa which Davies tells more than once.

30. See p. 171 below.

31. See *A Church Historian's Odyssey*, e.g., pp. 3, 9–10, 18–25, 102–104, 116–117, 140–141.

32. See *A Church Historian's Odyssey*, e.g., pp. 47, 51, 56, 89–90, 99–102, 108, 122, 142, 151–154, 203–206.

33. R. Kelso Carter (1849–1928), 1886.

34. See pp. 113–119 below.

Introduction II

In the second volume of Davies's sermons, *Preaching to a World in Crisis*, we have "Protests, Profound and Trivial: A Baccalaureate Address Given at Lehigh University, June 11, 1967." I was going to include this address in the present volume until I discovered that it had already been published. But what I cannot do without are evocative, compelling words:

> Let me conclude with a story that was told to me by a social welfare worker in South Africa. I lived in that land for six years where the racial problems are far more acute than in the deepest South of this country [the United States; these words were written in 1967]. The story is a parable. A pathetically poor and hungry African girl came to the welfare office for a glass of milk, her rickety limbs and her distended stomach proving she was a case of malnutrition. She was immediately offered a glass of milk. Before she allows it to touch her lips, she glanced across at her younger brother, and she asked: "How far down may I drink?"
>
> At this time, you will be drinking more interesting beverages than milk, perhaps the celebratory champagne. But as the goblet of opportunity is held in your hands, you must constantly ask, remembering the parched lips of God's underprivileged ones: "How far down dare I drink?"[35]

Yes, the story is a parable. Christianly, we are all cases of malnutrition. "How far down dare I drink?" Propriety. Consideration. Perhaps the younger brother needs milk, too. Is the glass half empty or half full? "How far down dare I drink?" Respect? Regard? Risk? Christianly, the privilege and the grant of grace constitute the challenge to dare to drink all the way down. We need no less.[36]

Davies concludes a sermon called simply "Immortality" with these words:

> And in that day of reunion, we shall be ashamed of doubts and fears, and falling on our knees, we shall exclaim "O Lord Jesus, king and Redeemer, your promises are greater than our dreams!"[37]

---

35. In the second volume of Davies's sermons, *Preaching to a World in Crisis*, we have "Protests, Profound and Trivial: A Baccalaurate Address Given at Lehigh University, June 11, 1967," pp. 168–174.73–174. This is another version of "The Cloister, and the Hearth, and the Community," and it is from this version that I quote the passage above. See *Preaching to a World in Crisis*, pp. 173–174.

36. I have turned the point of the parable from respect for the need of another to self-need. Perhaps the two needs are dialectically related—or wedded.

37. *Believing*, p. 148.

How Far Down Dare I Drink?

Promises greater than dreams. We need no less.

In sermons and out, Davies was ever entertaining these words of Paul: "But we have this treasure in earthen vessels, to show that the transcendent power belongs to God and not to us" (II Corinthians 4:7, RSV). He concludes his book, *Catching the Conscience*, with homage to Frederick Buechner:

> All Protestantism in general, and American Presbyterians in particular, can rejoice that in their midst is a man and a novelist who has found his calling as a minister of the Word of God to culture. But like most faithful ministers he deserves a wider congregation of believers and unbelievers to whom to proclaim the strange and searching ways of the grace of God, which only a humble and empty hand can accept, and by means of which the ordinary person becomes extraordinary.[38]

"Empty hand," "ordinary person becomes extraordinary": treasure in earthen vessels.

And here is the final paragraph of *A Mirror of the Ministry in Modern Novels*:

> The measure of the finest portraits of the ministry is that they show the reality of the temptations which assail the servants of God and the greatness of the grace which overcomes them. If the earthiness of the vessel is all they see, they are only caricaturists. If the treasure of the gospel alone is shown in their portraits, apart from the clay vessel, they are hagiographers and sentimentalists. But if they portray the ministry and priesthood in its squalor and grandeur, its earthiness and its treasure, they have succeeded in a most difficult and worthwhile enterprise. For the delineation of the squalor is a warning, and the portrayal of the grandeur is an encouragement which only the Christian artist can provide.[39]

Horton Davies was more effervescent, ebullient, irrepressible, engaging, and sparkling than these sermon texts can indicate. But we must be grateful to have them. They are indications, pointers, hints, and clues to a treasure in an earthen vessel named Horton Davies—and to that which he treasured.

---

38. *Catching the Conscience*, p. 161. See pp. 6, 100. Still writing on Graham Greene: "The great strength of the saints is that they who are ordinary become extraordinary through grace" (p. 103): treasure in earthen vessels.

39. *Mirror of the Ministry*, p. 186. See also, p. 103.

PART ONE

Responses To Gospel
A Yet More Blazing Certainty

FAITH

The Tide Turned

Transfiguration—Mount of Triumph, Mount of Defeat[1]

> And he came out and went, as his custom was, unto the Mount of Olives.
> (Luke 22:39)
>
> Then returned they unto Jerusalem from the Mount called Olivet.
> (Acts 1:12)

There is only one thing which these two texts have in common: the mention of the Mount of Olives. The rest is the greatest possible contrast.

In St. Luke's gospel, the drama of the Cross is reaching its ghastly climax. Jesus has left the Upper Room, preceded by the disciple who is to betray him. The master goes from the lighted security of the Upper Room to the dark uncertainty of the Mount of Olives and to the anguish and torment of the garden of Gethsemane. He walks the last few steps of the way of the Cross. The darkness of the scene is emphasized by the failure of the disciples. It is not only the treachery of Judas, but the cowardly denial of Peter, and the desertion of Jesus by all his disciples and friends. At the last, he stands alone. The crowds who have flocked to hear him will on the morrow cry, "Crucify him!" His teaching seems to have fallen on stony ground;

---

1. A curious order: one might expect first "Defeat," then "Triumph."

his good works of healing are ungratefully forgotten; even the few who should have carried out his work after him, the disciples, have left. It is as if his whole life's service was wasted, utterly worthless. He is like a pebble, it seems, that for three years disturbed the surface of the Sea of Galilee, and now the last ripple has died away. "And he came out and went to the Mount of Olives." He walked to his death and his defeat.

Now hear the second text that speaks of events weeks later. "Then returned they to Jerusalem, from the Mount called Olivet . . ." The disciples have left a scene of triumph, of glorious victory. For on the same mount, high above Jerusalem, the disciples have seen the vindication of Jesus. The mount of defeat has become the mount of victory.[2] The tide has turned. Read what had happened there. The risen Christ had said to these defeated, ashamed disciples, "But ye shall receive power when the Holy Ghost is come upon you; and ye shall be my witnesses both in Jerusalem and in all Judaea and Samaria and unto the uttermost part of the earth" [Acts 1:8]. And when he had said these things, as they were looking, he was taken up and a cloud received him out of their sight [see Acts 1:9]. The Mount of Olives was the mount of the ascension. From it Christ had ascended to the right hand of God, the father.

And this mount is a parable; it is a parable of faith. To the eyes of the world and even to the eyes of the disciples, the Mount of Olives was the mount of defeat. The mouth that had proclaimed the golden news of the kingdom was to be stopped; the hands that had blessed little children and folded the beloved-disciple John to his breast, that had been quick to heal the broken in body were to be nailed to the cross, transfixed and useless; the body in which God had been tabernacled for thirty-three years was to be crushed by the combined forces of evil. Man had done his vile worst. The messiah was murdered. Only one could look through the looming clouds and see the rays of dawn. Only one saw with the eye of faith, the victim, "Into Thy hand I commend my soul" [see Luke 23:46].

But, on the same Mount of Olives, by the almighty power of God, the messiah was to receive his greatest triumph.

In the sight of all the disciples Christ was taken to that throne that he had left for the Bethlehem stable. And his last words were a prophecy that the gospel he had committed to his friends to spread was going to be broadcast throughout the world. The hill of difficulty and defeat had become the hill of triumph. That is always God's way. He turned an instrument

---

2. See n. 1, p. 33 above.

The Tide Turned

of cruelty and injustice into the supreme means of loving-kindness. The ghastly gibbet of the cross has become the symbol of our redemption. The battle of goodness over evil was joined on the field of the Mount of Olives. It was there that supreme goodness was ignominiously defeated, where Satan and all his minions shrieked with triumph. On the same field, too, God won his greatest victory, the victory of the ascension.

And that is God's will for every Christian: to win his victory on the very field where he was previously defeated. Notice our Savior's last summons. They were to preach the gospel beginning at Jerusalem. It would have been much easier to start in Samaria, where they were unknown, where they had no stain on their character to wipe out. The difficult task was to proclaim the gospel in Jerusalem, where they had failed their Lord.[3] It required supreme bravery there to face up to the Temple authorities, the very people they had hidden from when Christ was betrayed. And yet, that was the right command to give them. "Conquer in Jerusalem," Jesus was saying in effect, "and you will have won the hardest battle; it will give you confidence to be my witnesses anywhere and everywhere."

"We must obey God and not men." Peter thought of the eagle-eyes of Annas and Caiaphas; he remembered the mockery of the servant-girl, "Thou also wast one of them."

How could he face these people again? He could only face them because his Lord was a risen and ascended Lord. They had divine power on their side. If God could wrench victory out of the crucifixion, he could make these cowards bold and resolute.

The Peter who denied Christ became Peter, the martyr, who died for Christ. He won the victory on the very field where he had failed so miserably, on the field of the fear of death.

Ruskin[4] tells us in *The Bible of Amiens* [1880–1885] of the marvelous designs and symbols on the great gateway of the cathedral. It shows representations of the apostles, with symbolic figures shadowing forth their distinguishing virtues and attendant frailties. Two emblems portray the character of Peter. Here is a man flying away from a tiger, Peter the craven, denying his Lord! Here is the same man riding the very tiger he fled, Peter the courageous, defying the might of the Caesars for his dear Lord's

---

3. See Arthur C. McGill, *Dying Unto Life: Arthur C. McGill on New God, New Death, New Life*, David Cain, ed. (Eugene, Oregon: Cascade Books, Wipf and Stock Publishers, 2013), Theological Fascinations, vol. II, p. 77, n. 3, p. 98, n. 21.

4. John Ruskin (1819–1900), distinguished British art critic, writer, and a painter himself.

sake, and later going bravely to a martyr's death. And between the two—the coward, flying from the tiger, and the hero, riding on the tiger—stands the Cross. The tragedy of Calvary, the wonder of the resurrection, the glory of the ascension, and the sublime mystery of Pentecost, intervene between Peter the Coward and Peter the Valiant.

What does this all mean for you and me? It means that we have to make our very failures the material of our successes. Let me give you one example, an important one. We all have a remarkable talent for believing that we are in the right; that is the spirit that engenders all our excuses and self-justifications. If business is not going well, the district is to blame, we will open elsewhere. If our health is not what it ought to be, we will change the doctor. If we are not altogether happy in the church we attend, we will change the church. We have never even faced up to the possibility that we are bad business-men or that we have refused to take the doctor's prescription. In the same way, have we seriously thought that many of our criticisms of the church are criticisms of ourselves?

Penitence is the beginning. You complain that the church is unfriendly. You are sensitive. Have you ever thought that your very reticence is the reason that has prevented people from making friends with you? Have you gone out of your way to make friends with the church? You complain that the sermons are over your head or the hymn-tunes unfamiliar. Have you ever thought that a sermon is meant to be the disclosure of God's revelation to you and that it demands that you should love God with all your mind [see Matthew 22:37; Mark 12:30; Luke 10:27] or have you thought that hymns beloved and familiar to you are stale and stereotyped for the new generation? We come to church to join God's family—and a queer lot of lame clucks they seem to be sometimes—but, if we are not happy, it is in all probability we who are to blame. We have not been prepared to enter fully into the fellowship. We remained on the outside edge and expected to be treated as friends.

My friends, before you can obtain the humility and charity that make up the real Christian, you must follow our Lord on both journeys to the Mount of Olives. Watch him praying, until the sweat on his brow is like great drops of blood [see Luke 22:44]. See him resolutely march to meet his betrayer, because he knows his cross is the price of the world's redemption. Go through these experiences with the humility of Christ, and it will give you an insight into the poverty of your spiritual life. At the foot of his Cross, you will cry like Peter: "Depart from me, O Lord, for I am a sinful man"

[Luke 5:8]. Or like Saul, you will say: "Who will deliver me from the body of this death?" [Romans 7:24].

You will know the answer as you stand on the same Mountain with the disciples. "Ye shall receive power," Christ will say to you, and "Ye shall be my witnesses" [Acts 1:8]. Immediately, the church will be transformed for you. It will be no longer the meeting place for religious ranks of simpletons. It will be for you the fellowship of the friends of Christ, the assembly of the saints, the trysting place of God with the very body of Christ. In its gatherings you will receive power from the Holy Spirit to defeat sin, suffering, and death.[5] You will be living in the strength of the risen Christ. The hymn says truly:

> What Christ bids me be
> He helps me to become.

For you the mount of defeat shall be the mount of triumph. "I can do all things through Christ that strengthens me." To him our king, teacher, master and Lord, be all glory and honor, world without end. Amen.

---

5. "Sin, suffering, and death"—this anti-Trinity—becomes thematic in Davies's sermons.

Death, Getaway of Life Eternal
The Adventure of *Analusis* (ἀνάλυσις)

EASTER SERMON

The time of my departure is at hand. (2 Timothy 4:6)

In nothing do we see a greater contrast between Christianity and other religions than in the teaching of Christianity about the life after death. In ancient Greece, heaven was the pale abode of disembodied spirits. Homer said it was the place where the heads of the dead shake and shiver. In remote Tibet and India, they believe in the transmigration of souls: a man must go on working out his salvation endlessly in one world after another. In Muslim Arabia and Turkey, sensual ideals prevail of heaven, which would be revolting to a Christian in this life. But when we turn to the New Testament, the nobility of the life after death is as sublime as it is certain. How triumphantly the early Christians rejoiced over Christ's resurrection and exulted over the life that is to come!

St. Paul uses a very luminous Greek word about death, as he awaits his expected end. "The time of my departure (*analusis*) is at hand," he says. What does this word mean? The exploration of this word's meaning is a voyage of discovery into the celestial country.

1. First, it was a seaman's word. It was used about unloosing a ship from its anchorage. As the apostle thinks about his approaching death, it's like the weighing of anchor, and sailing out on the sea of immortality. Isn't there something to fire the imagination here? John Masefield could sing of "the wheel's kick" and the "wind's song" and "the grey dawn breaking":

Death, Getaway of Life Eternal

> I must go down to the seas again, for the call of the running tide
> Is a wide call, and a clear call that cannot be denied.[1]

Surely the thought of launching out onto a voyage of discovery with our truest friend onboard, a cruise with Christ, presents a view of eternity much more attractive than the thought of "lying on beds of roses and meditating on the laws of Moses!" The late Sir J. M. Barrie[2] said: "To die will be an awfully big adventure." But what thrills an adventure brings! What variety! What unexpected joy! For this:

> From out our bourne of Time and Place
> The flood may bear me far,
> I hope to see my Pilot face to face
> When I have cross'd the bar.[3]

2. The word *analusis* is secondly a ploughman's term. It was used about unloosing a weary team of horses after a toilsome day. Paul had proved himself an indefatigable toiler. His life is a marvelous record of unflagging service. Now the rest that he deserved would be his. The tired animal, when he is set free, does not usually lie down, but canters about freely as if he had a new lease on life. It finds rest a different and voluntary occupation. The tired brain of the businessman is rested during golf. The rest enjoyed in heaven will not be a stagnant one. Henry Ward Beecher[4] struck the right note when he said that after death he would be "in the thick of things working for God and man." Blessed are the dead who die in the Lord, for they rest, not from all labor, as the Greek word suggests, but from exhausting toil.

3. The word for departure is also a traveler's word. It was used about "unloosing a tent," and continuing the march. "In my father's house are many resting places." They are stages on a further journey. The disciples

---

1. John Masefield (1878–1967), "Sea-Fever," *Salt-Water Ballads, The Poems and Plays of John Masefield*, vol. 1, Poems (New York: The Macmillan Company, 1923), p. 31. John Masefield was an English poet and writer and Poet Laureate of the United Kingdom, 1930–1967. *Salt-Water Ballads* dates from 1902. In "Sea-Fever," "I must go down to the seas again . . ." is repeated thrice, becoming thematic.

2. Sir J. M. Barrie (1860–1937) was a Scottish dramatist and the author of *Peter Pan* (1904).

3. Alfred Lord Tennyson (1809–1892), "Crossing the Bar," *The Works of Tennyson*, ed. Hallam, Lord Tennyson (New York: The Macmillan Company, 1939), p. 869.

4. Henry Ward Beecher (1813–1887) was an American Congregational minister and social worker.

were already in the father's house when they were in fellowship with Jesus. They had started on the road to God, but they had a long spiritual journey ahead of them. One day, they would fully know God.

4. Yet again, the word *analusis* is a philosopher's word. It signified the unloosing of a knot, the solving of a problem. Do you remember St. Augustine's fine saying: "A dead child knows all that has puzzled the sages"?

What mysteries hover over our daily pathway? Questions perpetually unresolved, knots that remained tied, skeins forever tangled and twisted. There is the early death of some promising young life; we shall go on asking without interruption, what was the purpose of it? There is the problem of undeserved suffering; why would cancer grip that unselfish gentle man in its deadly folds, like some grim snake? Why should that Battle of Britain pilot, shot down in the hour that he saved his country, go through life self-conscious about his burnt face? The injustice of these things cries out: "Why, O God, why, do you permit it?" There is again the problem of the prosperity of the wicked. Why do they seem to bypass bereavement, sorrow, and loss? Why do their enterprises always succeed? God's purpose, even though we cannot always see it, must be to make us trust him in the midst of darkness. But one day when "heaven's morning breaks" and "earth's vain shadows shall flee," we shall know the reason why.

We shall not only fully know our great redeemer, but we shall experience the rapture of reunion with our loved ones, and the broken family circles will be complete again. Let us therefore rejoice in the hope of the glory of God, and in the simple promise of our Savior: "If I live, ye shall live also" [John 14:19].

But this is a belief that must be accepted in the bottom of the heart, not merely in the top of the mind. We have not merely to believe in Christ.

Dr. Hubert Simpson tells of a New Zealand doctor summoned to the bedside of a dying gold-miner. He was beyond medical aid, but the doctor read to him from Revelation 21, the description of the heavenly city, Jerusalem. When he came to the words: "And the street of the city was pure gold" [Revelation 21:21], the dying man opened his eyes and exclaimed: "What's that? God in the streets? Has it been assayed, or are you only quoting from a promoter's prospectus?"

We know that this has been assayed, and that the promise comes to us from the lips of the man who tasted death. It is a crucified Christ who speaks the words: "I am the resurrection and the life" [John 11:25] and he points not to a remote heaven but beneath his feet to a shattered tomb. And I am prepared to stake my life on the truth of the promise of Christ.

PRAYER

O thou, God of the living and not of the dead, grant us the assurance that in the grasp of thy love, all is utterly safe; that our souls may commit unto thee our life and what is dearer far than our life; that, throughout eternity, in thy home, with thee, to thine own children never can harm befall, through Christ, the resurrection and the life. Amen.

Christian Certainties in an Uncertain World

A Colony of Heaven on Earth

A late spring sermon in South Africa

Thy Word is a lamp unto my feet and a light unto my path.
(Psalm 119:105)

At this time of year, we are making plans for our holidays. Where shall it be? Perhaps we'll go to Cape Town to coincide with the Van Riebeeck Festival[1]? Perhaps East London, where prehistoric fish swim the seas and incredibly ancient gentlemen stroll along the esplanade? Perhaps we'll go to the neon-lit splendor of Durban? If you have been to any of these places you will recall that they have one thing in common—apart from the sea. If you look out to sea on a clear day in each of these places you will see a steady white sentinel with brilliant golden eye towering over the waves, as steady as the rock on which it is built. You will not be able to see the lighthouse at midnight—but you will see its rays, like glistening torches penetrating the midnight blue, bringing warning to those who go down to the sea in ships and do their business in the great waters [see Psalm 107:23], bringing a comforting assurance of their bearings to the navigators!

The sea rages, darkness comes over the land, but the lighthouse stands and steadily the light is transmitted for the warning and the comfort of the sea's wayfarers. It stands immovable on the rock, solid in the flux and

---

1. The Boschendal / Jan Van Riebeeck Festival, launched in 1952, celebrating three centuries of white settlement in South Africa. Johan Anthomiszoon "Jan" Riebeech (1619–1677) founded Cape Town, 6 April, 1652.

change of the elements. This is a parable of the Revelation of God in the uncertain world of the atomic age. I would remind you this evening of the radiant certainties that flash forth from God's Revelation, making his Word a lamp unto your feet.

THIS IS GOD'S WORLD: HE MADE IT.

"In the beginning God created the heaven and the earth; and the earth was waste and void; and darkness was upon the face of the earth; and the spirit of God was upon the face of the waters. And God said: 'Let there be light, and there was light'" [Genesis 1:1–3].

This is not only majestic; it is true. And it has been true from the first instant of creation and every morning afterwards. Whether daylight comes peering through a port-hole on the high seas, or its roseate fingers transfigure the face of a sleeping child with holy innocence; whether it touches the pallid brow of a feverish patient or wakens campers in Kruger National Park[2] to the full flush and glow of life—whenever it comes, it is the finger of God who sends it! New every morning comes the promise that God neither slumbers nor sleeps. He remembers. Each day his divine first is renewed: "Let there be light!"

Ah! But there is more than that! He remembers the undeserving too, says our Savior. "He maketh his sun to rise on the just and on the unjust" [Matthew 5:45]. On the man who shakes his fist at the skies, on the very scoffer and cynic, is loaded daily the benefits of God. You may grudge your prayers to him, but he will not grudge you the gift of light. He gives with open hand, scattering light and life and loveliness. It is splendidly, gloriously given. Each day he says, "Let there be light and there is light." This is the first certainty: let it come home to your soul's eyes each morning. This is God's world. The light is his rapid greetings telegram, a celestial cable.

GOD LOVES YOU

But there is a yet more blazing certainty. God loves you; God is your friend.

This is the profoundest message that the lighthouse of God's Revelation flashes through the midnight hour of anxiety and suspense. Forget

---

2. A great game reserve and South Africa's first national park, 1926.

those fears and doubts, those worries and anxieties and listen to those who knew the eternal Son of God when he came to earth.

St. John, old and trusty servant of Christ exiled on the lonely fastness of Patmos, far from home and friends, declares, "Our fellowship is with the Father and with his son Jesus Christ and these little things we write that your joy may be fulfilled" [1 John 1:3].

Then here speaks another man who had good reason to doubt the existence of the light-house, for he had been ship-wrecked three times, imprisoned often, lashed, and stoned: he had been almost overwhelmed by the white horses of pain and buffeted to death in the sea of adversity. Yet St. Paul exclaims, "We give thanks unto the Father who made us fit to be partakers of the inheritance of the saints in light; who delivered us out of the kingdom of darkness and translated us into the kingdom of the son of his love" [Colossians 1:12–13].

And the only begotten son, he who had known at Calvary the sky of heaven clouded over with a leaden curtain and who cried with an agony of a child left alone in the darkness of an orphaned universe, "My God, My God, why hast thou forsaken me?" [Matthew 27:46; Mark 15:34] … he could say, "I am the light of the world. He that followeth me shall not walk in the darkness, but shall have the light of life" [John 8:12].

My brethren in Christ, do you realize what this means? Fathers and mothers here will know what it feels like to say goodbye to your sons, and wives and fiancées to say good-bye to your men when they left home for all the cruel hazards of war. Surely you can dimly guess the thoughts of God when men transfixed Jesus to the jagged Cross? But none of us can imagine the splendor of such love that God gave his son ungrudgingly, that his son should lay down his life for the sake of his enemies, for cunning Caiaphas, and procrastinating Pilate, as well as for the beloved disciple, John. Could God give you a deeper proof of his love than that?

I want you to cling to that tonight. Read every glowing promise of Christ, and remember that this only son whispered, as the cold blood clotted in his veins and arteries, as he died for you and your loved ones, "Father, into Thy hands, I commend my spirit" [Luke 23:46]. Father and Friend, our God!

Didn't our gloriously honest Savior tell us bluntly that a soul is saved, not by one cross only, but by two: his own and the soul's own?

Christian Certainties in an Uncertain World

A grand old Scots saint of the last century, Fraser of Brae,[3] had learnt that lesson. He records that whenever an untoward event clutched at his throat like a wolf in the dark, he thought, "This messenger is certainly hard-featured, but he brings me a love-token from the king." And the old saint asked himself, "What is this sent to teach me?"

It is sent to teach you your need of Christ. It is also sent to teach you sympathy with all the poor wounded and stricken hearts like yours. An outsider cannot help such; only those who have shared in the fellowship of the Cross and taken their crosses lovingly can help.

The lighthouse of God's Word flashes the sign of God's pity, loving-kindness, and tender mercy. "In him was life, and the life was the light of men" [John 1:4].

Its second message is that God is your father and friend, and Christ your elder brother. Heaven is your destination. There is a third promise that glows in the darkness: this is the light that scintillated from Christ's empty tomb, the fulfillment of his glorious promise, "If I live, ye shall live also" [John 14:19].

Gallant Paul, who had met the risen Christ on the Damascus Road, in a blinding flash of light knew the truth of that promise. He told his Christian co-workers never to be discouraged, "You are a colony of heaven." The king is there in residence. The world may seem to be enemy-occupied territory —it often is— but in the church of Christ the mopping-up operations have begun, and Christ on the cross, our glorious captain and commander, has already routed the three age-old enemies of man, sin, suffering and death. We are the agents of the king of kings who is in residence in heaven. The government shall be on his shoulder [see Isaiah 9:6]. When dejected at the apparent triumph of the enemies of Christ, lift up your hearts as you recall that in every corner of the globe are Christ's royal commissioners already aware of the everlasting glory and grace of the eternal kingdom. Yes, you are a colony of heaven.

During the recent war a returned British prisoner told a moving little story of his experiences in Germany. He and his friends in a prison hospital had been given a patch of earth to cultivate. They received from the Red Cross association packets of vegetable and flower seeds. In this enemy-occupied territory they made a garden with a giant sunflower that symbolized their aspiration of freedom. It grew until it was twenty-six feet high and it had a flower with a diameter of 12 inches. That garden was a

---

3. James Fraser of Brae (1639–1699). The "last century"?

colony of England in Germany. We, the members of the worldwide church of Jesus Christ, are a colony of heaven on earth.

That is the third message of God's revelation. Like Isaiah we claim, "Mine eyes have seen the king" [Isaiah 6:5]. And, in the knowledge of the certainty that God made us for eternal fellowship with him forever, we are steadied amidst the storms and tempests until we exclaim, "Wherefore we faint not; but though our outward man is decaying, yet our inward man is renewed day by day. For our light affliction which is for the moment, worketh for us more and more exceedingly an eternal weight of glory" [2 Corinthians 4:16–17].

How can we be sure of these things? Here is St. Paul's authority, "Seeing it is God that said light shall shine out of darkness, who shines in our hearts, to give the light of the knowledge of the glory of God in the face of Jesus Christ" [2 Corinthians 4:6].

HOPE

We Are Saved by Hope
The Victory in His Eyes
Sermon Delivered at Westminster Abbey in 1972

We are saved by hope. (Romans 8:24)

This is a text for the times! The Master of Balliol, in the concluding address on "The Challenge of Our Time," reminded listeners that they needed not only the Christian faith, and the Christian love, but Christian hope. Indeed, that was the basic necessity of our life. Here again, the Word of God is the Lord of life, as necessary to the nourishment of the soul, as bread is to the body. We are saved by hope. In *The Ballad of the Reading Gaol*, Oscar Wilde[1] points out that something was dead in each of us; and what was dead was hope.

But cries the modern man, bewildered and disillusioned, where can I find hope? Hopes are dupes. In 1919 we had exhausted all our resources, except hope; and that hope was a deceiver. It brought us to 1939. I have seen the world in ruins twice. Even now there are apparently responsible persons talking about World War III. We are threatened with the atom bomb, and before we have had time to realize the terrible possibilities that its discovery brings, there is news about a more diabolical weapon, the bacillus-spray. And you venture to speak to me of hope?

Yes, I do; but it is of Christian hope that I speak. To speak of self-generated hope, the hope of Mr. Micawber,[2] that something will turn up,

---

1. Oscar Wilde (1854–1900), "The Ballad of the Reading Gaol," 1897.
2. Wilkins Micawber in Charles Dickens's (1812–1870) novel, *David Copperfield* (1850).

would be nothing but an impertinence at this mid-century of crises, when the world is stunned and shocked by the course of events. It would be the sheerest folly, as well, in view of the destructive hatred and egotism that the Second World War has unleashed. Any man who has seen sin incarnate, whether it be only in the pictures of the Belsen victims with their dried and thirsty tongues, eloquent, even in death, of the sins of their fellow-men, or in the black crosses that are marked up on the ruins of Hamburg or Kiel in their hundreds, telling of bodies still interred beneath the debris of the dead cities, or in the callous faces of extortionists at home and abroad who condemn their brethren to die by their greed . . . A man who has seen these things, and a hundred other outrages against God and the children of God, has looked into the black heart of humanity and found little reason for hope there, except among the few. I repeat that I am declaring the Christian hope, not utopianism; a hope in God, not hope in men apart from God:

> Our God, our help in ages past,
> Our hope for years to come[3]

I want to remind you, that the Christian hope in God is a privilege. It is a privilege denied to those who pin their faith in men. For such, the world in which we live must be a veritable hell of despair. When Dante visualized hell, he saw it as the mortuary of hope. Over its grim, black entrance stood the fearful inscription, "Abandon hope, all ye who enter here." Many men are living in a world over which that inscription stands. St. Paul distinguishes the non-Christians as men "having no hope without God in the world." Do you remember John Buchan's[4] apt definition of the atheist as "a man who has no invisible means of support."?

When men have given up hope, they die. Many a doctor's surgical skill and medical attention have proved vain because the patient had lost hope, saw no purpose in living. Our amazing privilege, as Christians, is that we shall be perplexed, "yet not unto despair," for we know, over and above the sin of man, the triumphs of God's grace.

Over and above the change and decay all around, we see the renewal of the Holy Spirit; over and above the divisions of the nations, there is the unity of Christians of all races; over and above the inconstancy and fickleness of men, we have the God whose promises, sealed with the blood of the

---

3. Isaac Watts (1674–1748), "O God, Our Help in Ages Past," (based on Psalm 90).
4. John Buchan (1875–1940) was a Scottish writer and politician.

redeemer, cannot fail. Yes, "even though we are faithless, he cannot deny his nature."

The Christian hope is based on the constancy of God and his inflexible purposes. "Why art thou disquieted, O my soul?" says the Psalmist, and immediately supplies the answer "Hope thou in God" [Psalm 43:5]. "Let not your heart be troubled," says our Redeemer, "Ye believe in God. Believe also in me" [John 14:1]. William Wordsworth[5] tells in "The Excursion" of an old ploughman in the Lake District, who had weathered many storms, and at an advanced age continued his arduous work, with a rare spirit of content. He describes him thus, "A man he seems of cheerful yesterdays / And confident tomorrows." He had the grace of hope in his heart, daily renewed with family prayer and Sunday by Sunday in the village church. It was not the hope that springs eternal in the human breast, a hope of increased wages or of better times, no whistling in the dark here. It was the Christian hope that God is working his purpose out.

It is the same hope in God, and in the kingdom of God, that has provided cheerful yesterdays. And there can be no confident tomorrows unless we pin our hope in God, and in his Christ, who remains the same yesterday, today, and forever. He is the God of hope; that is one of his greatest titles, who out of defeat brings victory, out of a cross the resurrection, "We are saved by hope."

In the second place, the Christian hope is not only a hope for today and tomorrow, but for eternity. Our second privilege as Christians is our hope of eternal life.

Here again, we should be grateful for the solace that is ours compared with those who are not Christians. One of the most pitiful experiences in this life is to hear the uncontrolled sobbing of the unbelieving. There is no sorrow like that of the heart that believes Death is the last word on life, the cruel slamming of a door that remains forever bolted and barred. Compare that chilling experience with the rejoicing in the trumpet-notes of the gospel, "Blessed be the God and Father of our Lord Jesus Christ," which, according to his abundant mercy, hath "begotten us again unto the lively hope by the resurrection of Jesus Christ from the dead." "Begotten us again!" The words sound like the excited exclamations of a man who has been reprieved at the last minute from the execution, as we all have. And it continues, "to an inheritance incorruptible and undefiled, and that fadeth not away, reserved in heaven for you" [1 Peter 1:3–4].

---

5. William Wordsworth (1770–1850).

The liberation of that hope and the certainty of it! Our blessed Christ is the Columbus of the new world, opening up, by the voyage of the resurrection, undreamed of territories, and the fortunate isles of the blest! This Christian hope of resurrection gives the lie to despair! It closes the mouth of doubt. It gives a new lease on life to those who died young in faith and bravery; a reward to the martyrs and to the faithful unrequited in this life; and a promise of re-union to those who remain.

"We are saved by hope."

And this Christian hope is not only a comfort for the bereaved or the dying; it is a corrective to the cheapened totalitarian view of man that led to so much inhumanity. If, on that basis, you believe that man has only the utility value of 40 years of service to the state, then you are justified in controlling his life for the benefit of the larger entity, the state, which goes on for centuries after he is dead. This belief brings in its train the sterilization of the unfit, the ridding of the aged and infirm by euthanasia, and the abominable liquidation of revolutionaries or critics of the state. It is only the Christian belief in man, as destined to enjoy eternity with God, which gives him meaning and value. In very truth "we are saved by hope." And the lives of millions in the future in a planned world, where the individual may be sacrificed to the state, are in jeopardy without the Christian hope. For without it, they are cogs in the wheel of the state; but where it is believed, they are seen to have the dignity of souls destined for eternity.

In the third place, it is our privilege to be evangelists of hope. We, of all people, have no right to despair. "If God be for us, who can be against us?" [Romans 8:31]. But, we are too ready to forget that God is for us.

It is said that Luther's wife, noticing that the Reformer was dispirited and downcast, stabbed him awake with the question, "Have you not heard the news, terrible news? God is dead." Luther indignantly retorted, "How dare you blaspheme God?" She answered, with complete composure, "And if God is not dead, what right have you, his servant, to be so downcast and depressed?"

[It happened] when the Saracen hammered at the gates of hope and men said Christendom is lost. It happened at the Reformation, when the Church was more like the widow of Christ than his Bride. It happened at

We Are Saved by Hope

the Methodist revival when a dying Church heard on its deathbed the call to arise for "Thy Lord is come." It is going to happen again; the signs can already be seen in many a church where the chosen of Christ are bearing on their bodies and their souls the marks of the Lord Jesus, men and women literally broken and spent in suffering compassion for the world.

Heaven and earth pass away, our word never. Let us remember St. Francis and how the miracle of the resurrection happened for him. In all the gilded splendor of St. Peter's Rome, proud, ornate, boasting its wealth, he met a beggar exacting only a crust or a few remnants of food, and in his outraged soul he thought: the church cannot say, "Silver and gold have I none," therefore she cannot say, "In the name of Jesus Christ of Nazareth, rise up and walk" [Acts 3:6]. If the church takes up the name of Jesus and does not obey his commandments, it is dead, a gilded corpse. The time of the resurrection of Christendom is always when the Christian listens to the voice of Christ and obeys it, and amid all the uncertainties of human guides, it accepts the ringing challenge and the sturdy comfort of the risen Son of God.

If we were asked what the bedrock of our faith is, we should answer "faith in Christ." But there is something even deeper than that: Christ's confidence in himself. There are times when our faith wavers, and when, like the warrior on the field of Edgehill,[6] we say "I shall be busy this day; although I forget thee, do not forget me."

We stand most firmly not on our faith in Christ, but in the Lord's faith in himself. In one sad hour our Savior doubted the fidelity of man, "When the son of man cometh shall he find faith on the earth?" [Luke 18:8]. But faith in the gospel of the love of God never faltered or fainted. Here was a black moment on Calvary when the cry of a deserted soul broke from his lips [see Matthew 27:46; see Psalm 22:1]. It seemed awful to the innocent Son of God that truth should stand upon the scaffold,[7] but he did not doubt that it was truth that stood there. In the agony of our savior, the destroying fear that he was dying for a fiction never entered his soul. At the judgment bar of Pilate, with malicious priests, and an angered crowd outside, and a cowardly judge before him, he does not hesitate, "To this end was I born

---

6. Battle of Edgehill, Warwickshire, 23 October, 1642.

7. See "Once to Every Man and Nation," "Though the cause of evil prosper, yet the truth alone is strong; / Though her portion be the scaffold, and upon the throne be wrong . . ." The words were written in 1845 by James Russell Lowell (1819–1891).

and for this cause came I into the world that I might bear witness to the truth" [John 18:37].

I cannot exaggerate the steadiness that this conviction, the confidence of Christ, brings to us in the spiritual struggle. It heals, it fortifies, it inspires. When our own faith falters, we fall back on the faith of Christ. Then in the heat of the battle, panic creeps upon our spirits, and men about us are crying that all is lost, we lift our faces to the general of our salvation and the world's, and reassure ourselves with the victory in his eye. We need not only the gospel of Christ; we need the Christ of the gospel. We need to trust in the truth; but it is so much more helpful to trust in Jesus, the truth of God made flesh. We rest not only in the Sermon on the Mount, but in the one who preached it and lived it. We cling not only to the words that will never pass away, but to the Christ who will never pass away. We respond to his invitation, "Believe in me." Christ's confidence in himself is the ground of our confidence, if we would believe in him.

That God pities us; that is the abiding comfort of the gospel. It is not only love, but love incarnate. And the challenge and unspeakable privilege of the gospel is that it lives on in the world through "living epistles," not in printed words, but in obedient hearts, and lives, and actions that are the gospel and bring the assurance of faith to human tragedy, and love of God to human need, and the hands of Christ the healer.

Christian Realism
Uncontrollable Skidding in the Automobile of Life
Ash Wednesday, 1961

> In this World ye shall have tribulation; but be of good cheer, for I have overcome the World. (John 16:33)

Sermon notes.

The Saxon crucifix in Romsey Abbey[1] as the symbol of Christian Realism. The Leper Hospital in Pretoria —Christ's sufferings applied to human need. The Stations of the Cross painted by Sir Frank Brangwyn;[2] each of them valued at over $7,000 and in all worth $100,000. The correlation and connection between those two pictures, one of an English abbey crucifix, and of a South African leper hospital, is that of Christ, always adequate to human need.

Christ and Sin. Education is not the answer! We are each of us a private civil war, the ape warring with the angel in each of us,[3] and our tendency is either callousness or despair. But faced with the disappointed look of the world's Savior on the cross, callousness goes, and dazzled by the light of the resurrection, despair disappears.

---

1. Romsey Abbey, dating from the 10th century, in Romsey, Hampshire, England.
2. Sir Frank William Brangwyn (1867–1956) was an Anglo-Welsh artist.
3. See n. 28, p. 35 above.

Christ and suffering. Social Welfare and medicine are not the final answer. There are still cancer wards; still slums; still frustrations, fears, prejudices, bitterness. Christ does [three] things for us:

1. He takes the bitterness out of suffering.
2. He gives us a chance to show foul-weather loyalty to him.
3. He lets us learn sympathy.

Christ and death. It will take more than that to stop God!

Prayer

O God, whose beloved son Jesus Christ set his face aflint to go steadfastly to Jerusalem, the cross and the resurrection, give us such grace in Lent to confess him boldly before men, that he may acknowledge us to be his before thee.

Through the same Jesus Christ, our crucified, risen and reigning Lord. AMEN.

Christian Realism
Nassau Presbyterian Church, Princeton, April 26, 1959.

> In this world ye shall have tribulation; but be of good cheer, I have overcome the world. (John 16:33)

If you are an old-fashioned traveler who prefers to go by ship instead of air, and occasionally even to stretch your feet and limbs instead of merely using the ball of your feet on accelerators and brakes, then let us suppose we get off the ship at Southampton and take an afternoon's walk skirting the New Forest until we reach the ancient little country town of Romsey, dominated by the abbey church, with its Saxon foundations, its rounded and massive Norman pillars and its Gothic tracery, each quietly proclaiming the unhurried continuity of the Christian tradition. I ask you to notice one object only, unique in England. It is barely perceptible from the exterior, made of wood as grey as the stone and partly hidden by the climbing ivy. It is a Saxon crucifix. Beneath a little jutting chevron of a roof there stands the symbol of Christus Victor, Christ crucified, reigning from the tree.

What is different about this crucifix? Simply, that it depicts not a contorted figure, with broken arms and shattered legs, but one that stands upright and erect, above all, a figure of serenity. Above the victorious Christ can be seen another symbol. There is a pointing hand, the arm of which merges into a cloud, and which is saying, so we are to understand, "This is my beloved son, in whom I am well pleased" [Matthew 3:17; Mark 1:11; Luke 3:22].

To follow him is to understand, and to be upheld in understanding the nature of Christian realism. Perhaps I can best put it this way: the cross, its agony, its condemnation of the egotism of men, its proof of the costliness of choosing God's way when men mean to go their own, stands as criticism of all shallow optimisms. The resurrection, without which subsequent history of Christianity is unthinkable, with its martyrs known and unknown, its saints recognized and anonymous, this is the condemnation of all shallow pessimism. In the light of the cross, we know the worst about man: that he is a crucifier, a killer, whether his method be slow callousness, or passionate recrimination. In the light of the resurrection and God's vindication of his son and our Lord, we know that man is redeemable and his destiny not merely temporal, but eternal, and that is a criticism of ultimate pessimism. This is all summed up in the words of the divine realist himself, "In this world, ye shall have tribulation; but be of good cheer. I have overcome the world" [John 16:33].

Our problems: three answers: educational, political, religious.

In our problematic world of today there are three competing answers to the problems of human misery, anxiety, fear, hate, prejudice—all the jangled complex of human emotions.

One is the belief that our basic problem is ignorance and that education is the key to unlock it.

Every one of us here is committed to the belief in education, scientific, social, and humane, and glad that the privileged nations, educationally speaking, are sending their resources of information and personnel to the underprivileged nations through the United Nations' educational, scientific and cultural organizations. But granted the universal need of education, and of better education, will that of itself solve our problems? Will it solve moral problems? I say unhesitatingly, "No," because nothing is more dangerous to let loose in society than an educated brain who is a moral moron. Education can produce smart alecs and high-brow devils, whose unbridled and unprincipled egotism and conceit make them a destructive force in human society.

Let me give you a simple example of sophisticated selfishness. There was a junior high school teacher who had one brilliant pupil who came from a poor home. One day she was shocked to learn that her paragon had been breaking the school rules by running a private truck-stop in the recess. He was, shall we say, selling Coca-Cola to his class-mates at a considerable profit. He had a monopoly on the sub-teen market.

Reprimanding him, she had asked for an explanation. The future president of the local Chamber of Commerce replied: "I did it, because I'm smart and they're dumb." That very sentence is the epitaph of a moral education that is neutral, that recognizes duties neither to God nor to one's neighbor. Each one for himself, as the elephant said when he danced among the chickens.[1]

The second answer to our problems is that supplied by politics and the social sciences. In effect, it says, by a series of political, economic and social controls, we will change the natural and social environment of man, so that by means of legislation's restraints and the provision of various securities and amenities, barbaric man will become civilized man, discontented man will become happy man, and egotistic man will become altruistic man.

Not for a moment would I decry the need for better housing, the necessity for taxation to curb the monopoly of a firm or a person, and to make the basement of the poor man come much nearer the ceiling of the rich man; nor [would I decry] the work of the United Nations in settling or mollifying disputes that could easily make a cold war into a red-hot one. But again, I believe that however you improve the political, social, and economic structures of national and international communities, you have still evaded the fundamental problem of man; and that, like the educationalists, the politicians are guilty of a utopianism which does not do justice to the fundamental condition of man. "Power corrupts and absolute power . . ."

How is this crucifier to be redeemed? Let God direct your work under his government that your harvest be tender. Moreover, I believe that all human systems fail, not only in relation to the eradication of anti-social behavior and providing a satisfactory motivation for service. I believe they also fail because they have no answer to the problem of human suffering and death in the inviolable citadel of each human personality.

It is precisely at this point that education and politics have need of the aid of religion and, in our Western civilization, of the Christian religion.[2]

I ask you to notice that Christ, the eternal Son of God, is the answer to the egotism of man. To be confronted with his cross is to be confronted

---

1. See n. 29, p. 25 above.

2. Note this significant "Western" qualification. The point is not that Christianity is not ecumenical, but a door is here opened to other religions and other ways.

with the egotism of myself. It is my callousness (like Pilate's, my washing my hands of moral issues) that kills him; it is my fickleness and search for popularity that is mirrored in the crowd who cry exultant hosannas and so soon shout hoarsely for his crucifixion; it is my demand for visible proof which links me with doubting Thomas who must poke his fingers into the wounds of the nails and the spear and earns the rebuke, "Blessed are they that have not seen and yet have believed" [John 20:29].

Do I want God in a test-tube or a retort? He is indeed the undistorting mirror of my wizened little self, and yours. But his holy, uncomplaining, unresisting, and undeviating love is the compulsion to change this wizened being into one being transferred into his likeness. Didn't Paul say that "the love of Christ constrained" him? [2 Cortinthians 5:14]. It has constrained civilization itself in the West, throwing [around] monasteries and abbeys, prototypes of universities, hospitals, alms-houses, centers of worship and social services in Europe, the two Americas, and in the missions of Asia itself, placing their visible or invisible crosses[3] upon these social testimonies to the power of Christ over egotism?

Without a sense of indebtedness to Christ, it is difficult to see how any kind of social service can be devoid of pride, the insidious pride of philanthropy.[4] Patronage, for the genial humanist, is like the knowledgeable doctor, and humanity his mere patient or case, or the professor with his ignorant pupil, or the opulent lady signing a check in the slums. For the Christian man regularly decontaminated from pride in worship (for he recognizes that his common ground with all men is the need for divine forgiveness), for the Christian, it is the sacrifice of the Son of God for the wholly undeserving that produces the adoration that must issue in sacrificial service. Schweitzer[5] calls his life atonement, offering reparation to the Africans.

---

3. "Invisible crosses"—a stirring image.

4. See Arthur C. McGill, *Sermons of Arthur C. McGill*, ed. David Cain (Eugene, Oregon: Cascade Books, Wipf and Stock Publishers, 2007), pp. 8–9, 129. Davies and McGill were colleagues in the magnificent Department of Religion, Princeton University, in the 1960s.

5. This is of course the great Albert Schweitzer (1875–1965), theologian, biblical scholar, organist, physician, humanitarian. He was awarded the Nobel Peace Prize in 1953. I introduce Schweitzer in courses I teach—and I see a sea of blank faces. I ask, "How many of you have heard of Albert Schweitzer?" In a class of some seventy students, not one hand goes up. So I introduce Schweitzer and offer a lesson: fame is fleeting.

Christian Realism

I see the realism of the Christian faith and life in its attitude to suffering. Granted that modern medicine, and psychiatry, and social welfare can constrict and narrow the area of human suffering, they cannot eliminate it. There are still cancer-wards in our hospitals; there are still typhoons and hurricanes; there are still bitter personal disappointments and bereavements that can eat away the confidence of life like a corrosive acid on the heart. There will always be what humans describe as accidents, uncontrollable skidding in the automobile of life.

What then? Stoicism for the humanist, perhaps? For the Christian, the rare and inestimable privilege of entering creatively into suffering; for instead of becoming bitter, here is a chance to show a foul-weather loyalty to Christ, to stand by the Captain of his salvation when the ship of life lurches like a drunken man between low heaven and high water. Here too is the second chance to learn what sympathy means: literally suffering with others. Doesn't President Eisenhower's call for support for the Dimes for Hearts campaign reach us more surely because we know he is himself a cardiac case? Didn't President Franklin Delano Roosevelt's magnificent struggle against polio win our admiration because he knew what courage was? I submit that Christian realism enables the dedicated Christian to add his thorn of suffering to the crown of thorns of the crucified Christ and to be more loveable in his pain because he is one of (in the words of the poet Keats, himself a victim of tuberculosis) "those to whom the miseries of the world / Are misery, and will not let them rest."[6] When I meet such folk, I am ashamed to be so comfortable!

Attitude to death.

But the supreme realism of the Christian faith is seen in its recognition of death. It is our illusory way today to treat death as if it were a four-letter word unfit for polite ears, and to disguise funeral services as if they were family banquets. I sympathized with the protest of one of Noel Coward's characters in *Blithe Spirit*[7] who had asked how an acquaintance had died. A prune and prim type of lady, all angles and affectations, produced pe-

---

6. John Keats (1795–1821), *The Complete Poetical Works of John Keats* (Boston: Houghton Mifflin Company, 1912), "Hyperion—A Vision," Canto I, lines 148–149, p. 235 (1819).

7. Noel Coward (1899–1973) was an English playwright, actor, composer, etc. He wrote *Blythe Spirit* in 1941.

riphrases after periphrases until he burst out, "Don't say he passed on, or he passed over, or he passed out, or he is departed. Just say he died. He's dead, isn't he?"[8]

Christianity does not shirk the grim, inexorable reality of death. Each soul must pass through that single gate alone, absolutely alone. But it goes on to assert with sublime confidence it had learnt from the Christ who had returned from the no-man's land or frontier of death, "Neither life, nor death, nor things present, nor things to come can separate us from the love of Christ" [Romans 8:38–39[9]]. He himself with the nail prints in his hands, and the spear prints on his wounded side, who knew a long, acute, agony of death, assures us, "Let not your heart be troubled. Ye believe in God, believe also in me. In my Father's house are many mansions. I go to prepare a place for you" [John 14:1–2].

If this were not true, what are all you future educators, politicians, social scientists doing? You are only training one more generation of the prisoners of death, and the most you can do is to bedeck a gilded dungeon for them.

If, as countless generations of Christians have believed, with the evidence of the Holy Spirit within them, it is true, then your political, social and educational structures need to be tested by the mind of Christ; and you and those with whom you labor need that Christian realism which, in the gospel of the crucified, risen and reigning Christ, can overcome sin, suffering and death.

"In this world ye shall have tribulation, but I have overcome the world" [John 16:33].

---

8. Robert Warnock, *Representative Modern Plays, British* (Chicago: Scott, Foresman and Company, 1953), *Blithe Spirit: An Improbable Farce in Three Acts,*

9. Clearly, Davies is writing this from memory.

LOVE

Communion Address
A Cross in the Heart of God—That Crimson Love

> But far be it from me to glory, save in the cross of our Lord Jesus Christ, through whom the world hath been crucified unto me, and I unto the world... From henceforth let no man trouble me: for I bear branded on my body the marks of Jesus. (Galatians 6:14, 17)

As we prepare to meet our God in the blessed sacrament and trysting-place of his appointing, I would placard Christ before you and him crucified, to try to show you and myself what his life and death and resurrection mean, for us.

Do not isolate the Cross as one single all-important event; see it rather as the culmination and climax of God's visitation to the worthy sons of men. God has always been at his glorious work of redeeming fallen man, he sent his messengers in the patriarchs and prophets. Abraham's willingness to sacrifice his only son prefigured the sacrifice of Christ; Isaiah's prophetic picture of the suffering servant was a dim-foreshadowing of the Cross.

God sent the prophets, but at the end of the time of preparation, he sent his son. And from the moment of his birth on earth, this blessed Christ was the incarnation of the suffering love of God, costly in its self-giving from the Bethlehem baby's first bewildered cry to shriek of desolation from the depths of the cross. His whole life was God giving to the uttermost. Bethlehem, Nazareth, the wilderness, Galilee, Gethsemane, and Calvary, all roads lead to the cross.

Geoffrey Studdert-Kennedy said, "There was a Cross in the heart of God before there was a Cross on Calvary."[1] He was only repeating part of

---

1. Geoffrey Anketell Studdert-Kennedy (1883–1929) was an Anglican priest and

the sermon of Peter on the day of Pentecost, "Him being delivered by the determinate counsel and foreknowledge of God, ye, by the hands of lawless men, did crucify and slay" [Acts 2:23].

We see from this not only a gibbet on Calvary, but a wound in the heart of God from the beginning of time. He has a costly aching to deliver men and women from the bestiality, and terror, and cruelty, and indignity of their sins. "He was wounded by our transgressions" [Isaiah 53:5].

And yet this wounding of God, our shame, is also our greatest glory. St. Paul cries, "But far be it from me to glory save in the death of our Lord Jesus Christ" [Galatians 6:14]. St. Augustine cried in the same succession of the redeemed, speaking of Adam's disobedience, "O happy sin that gained so great and so glorious redemption."

And we all must say, "He loved me and gave himself for me" [Galatians 2:20]. This is the authentic evangelical experience. "Christ died for us while we were yet sinners." It is true. It is true for every child born into the world, beginning from its very nature to live for itself, taking to itself with grasping, if chubby hands, whatever is needed, as if it were its right. "Heaven lies about us in our infancy," says Wordsworth;[2] "Hell lies about us in our infancy," too. We are the products not only of God, but of the egotistical race of men. Needing redemption, our boast, whether we know it or not, whether our parents knew it or not, is this "Cross." Christ died for us—the redemption is waiting.

My friends, this is true throughout life. What dare I place my hope of salvation in, now and for evermore? That I am a minister? That I have had the privilege, during years of international conflict, of reading God's holy Word? In my friends and the good opinions of some of them? In my own faith in Christ? Ministers have fallen away from the faith. My very privilege as a minister can be a temptation to spiritual pride. My friends look up me with the eyes of charity, not with the piercing eyes of my Savior. Disappointed? I do not know what I shall have to face in this life; nor do you. But I know myself, and my weakness. But this I can be certain of, "Christ died for me." God's son came on earth to die for me. That is why I pin my faith

---

poet. Interestingly, Charles Allen Dinsmore writes, "There was a cross in the heart of God before there was one planted on a green hill outside Jerusalem," *Atonement in Literature and Life* (Boston: Houghton Mifflin Company, 1906), p. 232. Are they both indebted to Jakob Boehme (1575–1624)?

2. William Wordsworth (1770–1850), "Ode: Intimations of Immortality from Recollections of Early Childhood," *Romantic Poets: Blake to Poe*, ed. W. H. Auden and Norman Holmes Pearson (New York: The Viking Press, 1950), p. 199.

in the Cross, that crimson love, is unchanging, and Christ even now pleads for me before his father's throne. The chalice hidden beneath the table-cloth on the Lord's Table reminds me this morning that his blood availed for me; the broken bread reminds me that my Savior's body was broken by nails and butchered by sins, for me. That is why we can boast, not in our faith but in God's love.

A young minister lay dying in Manchester many years ago. His friends gathered round him and, in the intimate fashion of those days, asked how it fared with his soul. He answered that he was at peace. They then asked him, "Upon what do you ground your confidence?" He answered, "Upon oaths and promises and blood." Strange words? Not they, if you know your Bible. God is faithful to his promises. He stands by the oath he swore to our forefather Abraham, the promises he made through the prophets, the promises sealed by the redeemer's blood.

"Far be it from me to boast save in the Cross of our Lord Jesus Christ" but the quotation is incomplete, "through whom the world is crucified unto me, and I unto the world" [Galatians 6:14]. "From henceforth, let no man trouble me, for I bear in my body the marks of the Lord Jesus" [Galatians 6:17].

His cross demands our crosses. We may not boast of that, but it is our privilege. Our lives must show the owner's "stamp," or we are fakes. We must let him lay upon us his brand, his piercing stigmata. For St. Paul, it was illness, flogging, stoning, shipwreck, persecution, misunderstanding, entering compassionately into the suffering of others. For you the stigmata may be different. Many of you, I know and praise God for you, bear the stigmata in your souls: the owner's stamp: secret losses and disappointments, some agonies born uncomplainingly and lovingly, and in faith, some bitterness that you have conquered as a testimony to your beloved Lord's crucifixion. Other losses, other fears, will come. They, too, will be your honorable sores for him, whose broken body and shed blood is the pledge of our forgiveness and the inspiration of our sacrifice; and whose resurrection is the certainty of the victory of all who follow in his train.

Let me give you profound instance of how one soul responded to the Cross. It was told by George Adam Smith, great Principal of Aberdeen University,[3] but a very humble Christian. He once was traveling in a train with a young Romanist priest about to set sail as a missionary to a part of

---

3. Sir George Adam Smith (1856–1942), Scottish theologian and scholar of the Hebrew Bible. He was principal of Aberdeen University from 1909 to 1936.

Africa where a white man's life was reckoned not by years, but by months. He was on his way to bid farewell to his mother forever upon this side of the grave. Adam Smith reasoned with him, agreed that he must give up his life whole-heartedly and without reservation. "But" he said, "Why throw it away? Why not use it for long years in his service? Wouldn't it be better for Christ's sake to think it over again?" Even as the train stopped and the young missionary alighted, Smith still leaned out of the window and still pleaded with him. The young man simply smiled and then lifted up the crucifix he wore, looked at it lovingly, and answered, "He loved me and gave himself for me. And I, can I hold back?"

So the risen and glorified Savior with the wound-prints in his hands beckons you to follow him, in costly compassion, in courageous witness, in accepting your share of redemption through the loving facing of pain and loss, and you, can you hold back?

The Christian Motive
The Love of Christ Constrains Us

The love of Christ constrains us. (2 Corinthians 5:14)

What is the motive of Christian service? What built our medieval cathedrals with their graceful spires or climbing towers, with their miraculous rain-bowed windows, their embossed roofs and fan-tracery? What drove Bach to write his *St. John's Passion*,[1] and Handel to compose his *Messiah*[2]? What sent Livingstone[3] into the dark and treacherous heart of an unknown continent? What drove Elizabeth Fry[4] to the vermin-infested prisons of England day after day? What sent Ignatius,[5] an octogenarian, manfully to face the lions in the Roman arena? What makes hundreds of thousands of believers the world over to worship, each Sunday, and to their knees each night? What is the power that enables men and women to face suffering, bereavement and catastrophe unshaken and still confident? What is the motive of all sacrifice and unselfishness?

There can only be two answers. It is either fear, or love. There is a famous Latin saying quoted with approval by the atheists: *timor fecit deos*. Fear made the gods. Is this the truth? Is that the last word in explanation of

---

1. Johann Sabastian Bach (1685–1750) wrote *St. John's Passion* in 1724.
2. George Friederich Händel (1685–1759) composed *Messiah* in 1741.
3. David Livingstone (1813–1873). Henry Morton Stanley was sent to search for Livingstone and found him in the town of Ujiji on Lake Tanganyika in the autumn of 1871. Upon encountering him, he may have uttered the famous words, "Dr. Livingstone, I presume."
4. Elizabeth Fry (1780–1845), "angel of prisons."
5. Ignatius of Antioch (c. 35-c. 107).

How Far Down Dare I Drink?

the Christian faith? Granted that the primitive savage cowering in his cave on a midwinter midnight endued the shrieking wind with supernatural powers, and thought the lightening that struck the tallest fir-tree in the forest to the ground was a god. But we are speaking of twentieth century faith, of the mature Christian faith. Is this the product of fear?

Is the schoolboy's conception of God the right one? You remember he said, "God is the sort of person who is always snooping round to see if anyone is enjoying himself; and then trying to stop him." Is he [God] the celestial policeman and judge anxious to entrap man and to sentence him to everlasting torture and punishment?

And are we Christians to avoid eternal misery in hell by going to church and paying our collection for a fire insurance policy? That is an unworthy caricature of our Christian faith. But it would be equally wrong to go to the other extreme, and to suggest that the motive of our faith is sentimentalism, that we are poor miserable failures in the real world of men and affairs, who come to confide in a benevolent heavenly friend, an indulgent heavenly grandfather with a benign smile and a pocket full of comforts. Indulgent, he is not, as we have found in the discipline we have to bear, and in the great demands he makes upon us, and as we know to our cost through unanswered prayers.

We might have come to God looking for an ally, a conspirator: but we leave knowing that he is a master and a judge to whom we must submit.

It was not a cry of fear that inspired the Hallelujah Chorus, no more than it was sentimentalism that drove Livingstone through infested swamps, and untrodden paths in thick tropical jungles . . . and other nameless obstacles.

No, we could all sincerely say with the great Catholic missionary, St. Francis Xavier[6]:

> My God I love Thee; not because
> I hope for Heav'n thereby,
> Nor yet because, who love Thee not
> May eternally die.

> Then why?

> Thou, O my Jesus, Thou didst me

---

6. St. Francis Xavier (1506–1552) was one of the founders, in 1534, of the Society of Jesus.

The Christian Motive

Upon the cross embrace;
For me didst bear the nails and spear,
And manifold disgrace.

And griefs and torments numberless,
And sweat, of agony,
E'en death itself; and all for man
Who was Thine enemy.

Then why, O blessèd Jesus Christ
Should I not love Thee well? . . .[7]

The answer is St. Paul's, "For the love of Christ constraineth us; because we thus judge that one died for all, therefore all died; And he died for all that they which live should no longer live unto themselves, but unto him who for their sakes died and rose again" [2 Corinthians 5:14–15].

The motive of the Christian life is not fear of God, nor the desire to make God our ally, nor our desire for the spiritual well-being of mankind, nay, it is not even our love for Christ. It is simply and solely and uniquely his gracious love for us sealed in his own blood on the cross. That has built cathedrals and villages, Bethel's inspired artists, musicians, and poets, sent forth missionaries, social workers, empowered apostles, and prophets, and martyrs. "The Son of God loved me and gave himself for me" [Galatians 2:20]. The motive of all our Christian life is but a glad response to God's self-giving in Christ. It is not fear, but love.

"For the love of Christ constraineth us." Look at that key word—"constraineth"—for a moment. It is not the compulsion of force, it is the cogency of love. Dr. E. P. Dickie suggests that the Greek word for "constraineth" is a technical one used of rowers in a galley. It suggests a man who commands and gives the timing to the rowers.

St. Paul, when he used the words, may have thought of one galley famous in Grecian history. The island of Mitylene had revolted from the city-state of Athens and was at length subdued. The Athenians in their madness dictated bloodthirsty terms to the islanders. They decreed that the entire male population should be put to death, and the women and children were to be sold as slaves. A galley was to be sent out to carry out the hateful revenge. Then wiser and gentler voices were heard in council,

---

7. 17th century; trans. Edward Caswall (1814–1878); Edward Caswall was an Anglican clergyman and hymn writer. He became a Roman Catholic.

the motion was defeated, and the decree cancelled. Another galley was sent to declare the juster peace terms. Could they arrive in time? The lives of thousands depended on their reaching the island first, and the other crew had twenty-four hours' start! The men bent to their oars driven on by the urgency of their errand. They ate as they rowed, and snatched only a few hours' sleep in turn. When the island hove in sight, the barbarous decree was already being read out to the terrified islanders. But they were in time to save the massacre. "Luckily," says Thucydides,[8] the historian, "they met with no contrary wind, and the first ship made no haste on so horrid an errand." It was not force that constrained these magnificent rowers. It was not the lash of their overseer that drove them on, it was love, love for their fellow-men, though until lately their enemies. That is strong compelling power. But not the most powerful, because we humans know each other too well. We, changeable creatures made up of profound pity alternating with cold indifference, cannot keep such devotion at white-heat. There is a great dynamic in Christ's love for us. It is Christ on Calvary that wins our hearts' allegiance.

This love commands sorrow at the hurts done to love. Do you remember C. E. Montague's[9] *Rough Justice* and his description of the boy who was taken to church for the first time. He heard of the death of Jesus and he wondered how the people in the congregation could remain so unmoved. He thought they could not realize the cruelty of it all. When the service ended, he ran off into the shrubbery to cry. The heroism in the death of Christ stirs even the pagan to admiration, but there is more here than the death of a human martyr. It is the death of the only-begotten and innocent Son of God, slain by the sins of men. It is the effusion of the blood from God's own heart, and in the presence of that Cross man knows himself to be loved at a great cost. Christ did this for him, what can he do for Christ?

> "Three things there are" said one
> "That miracles are."
> Dawn and the setting sun
> And a falling star.
>
> "Three things there be" he said—
> "Beyond man's quest:
> The white peace of the dead

---

8. Thucydides (c. 460-c. 395) was a Greek historian and author of *The History of the Peloponnesian War*.

9. Charles Edward Montague (1867–1928) was an English journalist and novelist.

And a heart at rest."

"One only thing," he cried
"Draws all men still—
A stark cross standing wide
Upon a windy hill."[10]

That is not all. Because of Bethlehem, because of the agony in the wilderness, because of the holy cross and the glorious resurrection, "the love of Christ constrains us."

---

10. E. P. Dickie, "Postscript: 'If I Be Lifted Up'" (John 12:32).

JOY

A Talk on Carols
The Original Merry Christmas
Sunday, 27th December, 1942, 4:00 p.m., Wallington.

A little girl was an ardent listener to the wireless radio. One day, she was taken to church for the first time. When she was at dinner, her parents asked her how she liked the service. She replied, "I liked the music better than the news." This afternoon you have heard the news in the music. And the rest of the bulletin is about music. I'm going to try to answer the question: How did we get our carols? The answer is: in many ways, some of them very surprising.

(1) Some of oldest and loveliest carols have the jolliest tunes—not solemn enough, it would seem, to have been written for church services. Indeed they were not composed for church purposes, but for Christmas parties. And the tunes were merry because they were accompanied by dancing.

I suppose that at the family festival the young boys and girls danced and the older fathers and mothers and aunts and uncles sang the jolly accompaniment. An old writer, Barnaby Googe,[1] gives us a lively picture of Christmas festivities that were held in an English church during the reign of Queen Elizabeth. It is contained in a poem, thus:

---

1. Barnaby Googe (1540–1594) was an English poet and translator.

How Far Down Dare I Drink?

> Three masses every priest doth sing
> Upon that solemne day,
> With offering unto every one
> That so the more may play;
> This done a wooden child in clowttes
> Is on the altar set;
> About the which doth boys and girls
> Do daunce and trimly jet:
> And carols sing in prayse of Christ
> And for to help them heare,
> The organs answer every verse
> With sweet and solemn cheer.
> The priests do rore aloud;
> And round about their parents stand
> To see the sport and with their voyce
> Do helpe them and their hand.[2]

So that dancing, singing and acting of Nativity plays were all part of the church's celebrations of the glorious birth of God's glorious son.

(2) Carols also came to be written in another way. You will remember that in the poem I have just read you, mention was made of a wooden doll that was set upon the altar. Most of the carols of the various nations were written to be sung around a crib which was set up in the church during the Christmas season. Francis of Assisi,[3] who called himself one of God's merry men,[4] is said to have started the practice.

(3) A third way in which carols arose was this. They were part of the miracle plays or mystery plays or morality plays, which are the foundation of our modern drama. These plays were new ways of spreading the Christian teaching inspired by the church. Plays were given based either upon stories from the Bible, or from the lives of the saints, or from common life in which virtues or vices appeared as stage characters.

These plays, like the carols often included in them, were composed by the working-people. For instance, at York, in the 16th century, fifty of

---

2. Barnabe Googe, "Popish Kingdom," Book IV (1570) in Arthur Henry Bullen, *A Christmas Garland* (London: John C. Nimmo, 1885), pp. 271–277. Spellings of "Barnabe Googe" vary. A. H. Henry (1857–1920) was an English editor and publisher.

3. St. Francis (c. 1181–1226) founded the Franciscan Order in 1210.

4. I am reminded of the wonderful words of the Curé de Torcy in Georges Bernanos's extraordinary novel, *The Diary of a Country Priest*: "The opposite of a Christian people is a people grown sad and old"—George Bernanos, *The Diary of a Country Priest*, trans. Pamela Morris (New York: The Macmillian Company, 1937), p. 21.

A Talk on Carols

these plays were performed in the course of the Christian year. The Guilds of the city combined to perform them. At Chester, as many as twenty-four plays were produced in one day. They were acted on the tops of carts, which were wheeled down the streets. The audience was the street-bystanders; they stood still whilst the various acts or scenes of the play moved on to meet them.

Sometimes the subject-matter of these plays was very appropriately allotted to the guilds who had the facilities for providing the scenery and the equipment. For instance, the water-drawers of the Dee at Chester played "The Ark and the Flood," whilst the shipwrights of York built the ark, and the mariners played the parts of Noah's sons. The chandlers were responsible for producing the star in the East; and the goldbeaters provided the three gifts of the wise men; the vintners produced the miracle of Cana in Galilee turning the water into wine, whilst the bakers were responsible for the bread in the representation of the Last Supper.

These plays were ultimately suppressed because too much comedy was introduced into them. For instance, the Noah's Ark play at Chester was a rollicking success. The chief joke was that Noah's shrewish wife refused to enter the Ark and finally, after a lot of back-chat, she was carried in protesting by Noah and all his sons.

These plays were often enlivened by singing. The Coventry Christmas play allows for songs of joy by the angels, the shepherds, and the singing of a lullaby by Mary.

(4) Carols also came to be written in a fourth way. Poets at Christmas time would augment their meager pittance by writing carols. These would be printed off on broadsheets and sold to passers-by at fairs. They were a kind of musical Christmas card.

But of course the first inspiration of all Christmas carols was the first Christmas carol itself.

Its inspiring words were sung from the sky. These are preserved, but not, alas, the tune.

Christmas carols flourished throughout the middle ages. They were very popular in the reign of Elizabeth and James I. But when Cromwell came into power, he, with the full concurrence of the Puritan ministers, put a ban upon Christmas festivities. As Christmas day was not observed as a special day of thanksgiving, the carols went too. No longer sung in the churches of Commonwealth England, they were sung in the public houses. With the Restoration of the monarchy, came the restoration of carols. But

How Far Down Dare I Drink?

the Puritan prohibition lived on in Scotland—where the Ministers said that since every Sunday celebrated the Lord's birth, death, and resurrection, why have a special celebration of part of Christ's life on one day? The objection was very logical and the Scots, being a logical people, accepted it. And to this day, Puritan Scotland makes holiday at New Years' time instead of at Christmas.

The best old carols ever sung by the English people were discovered only in 1850. They were found in a common-place book in a worn manuscript hidden behind a book-case in Balliol College Library, Oxford. In this book, a London grocer records all the things he didn't wish to forget between the years 1500 to 1530. There are included tables of weights, dates of fairs, cookery recipes, children's births, notes on the breaking in of horses and the brewing of beer, with riddles, puzzles, and poems in English, French, and Latin, and a number of carols. Most of these have found their way into the famous *Oxford Book of Carols*,[5] the finest collection in our language.

All this information I have given you makes me wonder if we have lost the original merry Christmas celebrated with singing, dancing, and acting, and whether we worship at this time the man of sorrows acquainted with grief, not him who said, "I am come that they might have life, and have it more abundantly." I wonder.

---

5. Percy Deamer, Martin Shaw, Ralph Vaughan Williams, anthologists. (Oxford: Oxford University Press, 1928).

Triple Victory
The Flag Blown Taut
Easter Sunday, 1944

> He showed himself alive after his Passion. (Acts 1:3)
>
> Hallelujah, for the Lord God omnipotent reigneth. (Revelation 19:6)

Easter Sunday is the greatest day in the church year and the first Easter day is the greatest day in the history of the world. Why is this? It is because it sounds the last "all-clear" of God's victory, after the terrible siren of crucifixion. It is a clear, persistent note of reassurance, after the tremulous fearful, hesitant, quavering of fear. There was no siren sounding in the ears of our Lord, it is true, but the disciples heard it and took cover. And Easter day was the day of their hope, the day the last all-clear sounded for them. Easter day is victory day, for the disciples and for us. When Jesus showed himself alive after his Passion, the sirens ceased to wail, and the all-clear banished their fears. After that, the all-clear was forever sounding in their ears, there were still to be sirens (the terrible sirens of persecution), but the disciples heard continually the Victory note, "Hallelujah, for the Lord God reigneth," "He is the king of kings and Lord of lords," cried the church, which was being crucified under Nero.[1]

Victory is the best word for describing the meaning of the resurrection for us today. Victory! That lets us into the secret. Victory! What does it mean for you? It means the church bells ringing in every steeple in England and the colonies; it means flags flying from the town halls of England, butting across the streets, children waving their shilling union jacks, old men

---

1. Nero (37–68) was Roman Emperor from 54 to 68.

glad that they have lived to see this through, young men abroad rushing to the telegraph offices to wire greetings home, and women at home crying with relief and joy. It means that and so much more to us all.

So the disciples felt that joy and that relief because a cosmic victory had been won. The most gigantic battle of all of the demonic forces against God had resulted in an eternal victory. They would have other battles to fight, but the campaign was won. God as man, Jesus Christ, was back from the war.

He had crossed the frontier of death and he had come home.

Their Christ, God the son, was home from the World-War. Now they knew they could shout, "O death, where is thy sting/ O grave, where is thy victory?" [1 Corinthians 15:55; "victory" precedes "sting"]. No need for them to speak of death, as the country from whose [boundary] no traveler returns. "He showed himself alive after his passion." The victim of the Cross was the victor. The sacrifice of the cross was not wasted. Nothing good is wasted in the universe over which God reigns. The cross is the victorious cross. Christ returns alive after crossing the frontier of death. God wins; if we are on God's side, we win.

This was a triple victory; it is now.

This is God's victory over fear of death. "If I live, ye shall live also" [John 14:19]. He lives; he is the God of the living, not of the dead [see Mark 12:27]. Fear not them that kill the body, but rather them that kill the soul [see Matthew 10:28]. These words of promise were all spoken by a risen Savior, by the living God who'd been in the forefront of the battle, between death, and sin, and suffering, and fear, and himself, and came back. He had come back over the frontier of death. Nails, spears, and a cross. Today bombs, mines, torpedoes, and shells. The same death. But death has lost its sting since Jesus crossed the river. Fear not death, because he has conquered death.

"Rather fear those that can kill the soul," said Jesus. A far more terrible thing is sin. We have seen in our time a country deliberately set up the standards of Satan as its ideal. We who thought human nature was getting better and better, have seen nations snap their fingers in the face of God. Let me quote you the words of an ex-Nazi, who was the president of the Danzig Senate. Herman Rauschning[2] says:

---

2. Herman Rauschning (1887–1982) joined the Nazis briefly before breaking with and denouncing them.

Triple Victory

In Nazism, there stands revealed the anti-human and anti-Christian nature of a purely this-worldly order. A generation is growing that can only be regarded as devilish, a generation to which all that is humane is alien; men planned like machines, to whom any idea of an authority outside of themselves is absurd. Nazism is the subtlest and most consistent attempt in history to make political profit out of the evil in men and out of evil men. True to its leader's book, Nazism appeals to the lowest instincts of humanity.

Now don't think you are answering me if you say, "But there are evil men in England." This devilishness in Germany is the official policy of the country—the basis of its education, the reason for its Gestapo and its concentration-camps. This is organized rebellion against God.

That is the thing to fear: sin. There is only one way for men and nations to be rid of the fear of such sin: to fight it now with its own weapons and to fight it in their own hearts with their faith in Christ.

The victory over sin has also been won by Christ. The Nazis and the Japanese might conceivably have fought their way over the English dead in London; but they will not fight their way across the frontiers of death. God keeps the post.

But this victory of Christ over sin has to be appropriated in this world. By the insight God has given us, we and our allies will conquer the foes of God. But we shall have to uproot Nazism—deliberate organized evil—in this country. That can be done only if this country becomes a positively Christian country.

Today, we remember that Christ defeated the devilish power of evil. We need the penitence, the holy love, that Christ may win his victory over us and our friends and neighbors, that a cosmic victory may become a crusade in England. The world-wide campaign is won; our spiritual campaign is only beginning. The resurrection shows that the universe is on the side of right. Let us see that, Christ helping us, we are on the side of the universe. Christ has saved us.

Christ's resurrection is the victory over suffering.

Have you watched a flag in the breeze? The wind curls it up round the pole so that you cannot make out its emblem. Then the wind changes; a breeze blows it out taut; and you make out the design. The resurrection blew the flag taut, and the world saw in that divine instant that the Cross was the world's pattern. God, by entering into our human suffering, showed that was part of his design for the universe.

Christ has conquered suffering for his friends because they know that this is the path he walked along to victory. They are making up what is lacking in the sufferings of Christ; they know the most intimate fellowship with Christ, because they have dedicated the hardest thing in life to God. "This," they say, "is the price I pay to prove my faith." They know that those who suffer with him shall reign with him. They live in hope, nay in certainty that the sufferings of this life are not to be compared with the joy that shall be revealed [see Romans 8:18].

The cross is the price; the resurrection is the reward. That is God's plan. For them often the flag curls despairingly round the flag-pole. But in the resurrection, the wind of God blew out the flag, and they know they have entered into the purpose of God, through suffering to eternal life. This is their victory-day.

This is our triple victory: the victory of God over death, sin, and suffering.

The risen Lord comes to meet us from the dark frontier of death, "If I live, ye shall live also, and all my disciples" [see John 14:19]. He returns from the fray with [doing battle against] demonic will, "I have overcome the world" [John 16:33]. And so will you with his power.

He returns from the agony on the Cross with nail-prints, and spear-scars, and he says, "Follow me" [Matthew 4:19; Mark 1:17].

Let us pray:

Victorious God, who for our redemption didst give thy only-begotten son to the death on the cross, and by his glorious resurrection hast delivered us from the power of death and sin and suffering, grant us evermore to live with him in the joy of his resurrection; through the same Jesus Christ, our Lord. Amen.

The Two Census Books
Income Tax, Outcome Tax

There went out a decree from Caesar Augustus, that the entire world should be enrolled. (Luke 2:1)

They which are written in the lamb's book of life. (Revelation 21:27)

The two texts speak of two census-books, two registration files. Sometimes we speak as if registration were simply a modern disease, an invention of a bureaucratic government with an insatiable delight in red-tape. And as we gaze in bewilderment at the varied information required of us, we feel like imitating the baffled Negro who wrote across his national registration form in bold capitals, "When I'm wanted, I'm here!" It is some comfort to know that ancient governments required the same of their subjects.

In fact the very first of our texts reminds us that Joseph went up to Bethlehem to be registered. Caesar Augustus demanded that the people should each go to their native places. When arrived there, they were expected to give details of their family. This was not a registration for national service. It was a primitive way of collecting income-tax.

You will remember that hardly had Joseph and Mary reached Bethlehem, when Jesus was born. This enrollment form was therefore the first book in which the name of Jesus Christ was written.

The other census book stands at the end of the gospel. It is a book written in heaven. This time Jesus's name is not an insignificant entry in a file of the emperor's. His name is on the covers of the book of destiny. It is his book. And of all the glorious names with which he has been honored by

How Far Down Dare I Drink?

men, he selects the name of the Lamb. His tenderness and readiness to bear suffering are his chief characteristics.

Think of this then: the gospel of the incarnation begins with the name of Jesus being written among the people living in the world, written there almost as soon as he was born. It is written among the facts of the world's history. No doubt the official entry reads, "Jesus, male child, born to Mary, wife of Joseph, at Bethlehem."

Strange that this insignificant entry should be the event from which we date the world's records. Every time we write a letter, or make a payment in a ledger, we testify that a change came for the world when Jesus was born. Human history began again then. The years before counted only as a mere preparation; they were a mere curtain-raiser before the drama of redemption takes place: merely B.C. This was the greatest event in human history: *Magna Carta*, the battle of Waterloo, the two Great Wars, they are nothing in comparison with this epoch-making event when the Word became flesh.

Have you ever tried to think what our lives would have been like if this event had not been recorded in the census-book of Caesar? It is impossible. Take away all our charitable institutions, almshouses, hospices with their significant red-crosses, and poor-houses. With them, remove all our reformers: Wilberforce, Elizabeth Fry, and Charles Kingsley. Eradicate the poems of Milton, Donne, Traherne, George Herbert, William Cowper, Gerard Manly Hopkins, T. S. Eliot and the rest. Tear out the compositions of Handel, Bach, and Purcell from your music-books. Remove the Bible and *The Pilgrim's Progress*[1] from your library shelves, with many others. Go in our art galleries and remove the canvases of all the Italian masters from the walls: Michelangelo, Raphael, and Titian; clear away the Flemish work of Rembrandt, the Spanish work of El Greco, the English work of Blake. Do all this, and you will have stripped life bare of its most glorious enrichments.

But even aesthetics are not essential to life. Remove Jesus from the family and the bond of union is dissolved. Respect, sympathy, sacrifice, have fled from life. The cradle of Jesus has proved to be the cradle of the world's true hopes and joys. Most of our consolations in this world and our visions of a better world beyond were borne of Christ's coming. Remove the risen Lord from life, and you cramp the universe. You limit life to the narrow and bleak cul-de-sac of death; you confine man to his own puny efforts, and the lever of God cannot lift him from the mire.

---

1. John Bunyan (1628–1688) published *The Pilgrim's Progress* in 1678.

Take Jesus from life and the world is color-blind; the instincts of lust, greed, rapine, and murder speak for the animal in us. The spirit is silent, because in dethroning Christ, you have murdered it with your materialism. The first census-book records the only world-shaking event when eternity burst into time, and God spoke his final word to man.

The other book is at the end of the gospel, "They that are written in the Lamb's book of life." What is the end of all our life? What is the purpose of this human drama in which we all play our parts? The end of it is that a people are to be gathered home to God, a people whose names can be written down as alive. It is the Lamb's book of life.

Which is the more important of the two books? Which has to be reckoned now? The census-book of Caesar has perished; the lamb's book of life remains. It was an accident of circumstance that determined whose lives were to be written in Caesar's book. It is merely a contingency of time that my registration number is KBKE 76.10. What does this matter when the whole of human history is under review? But it is no accident that decides whose names are written in the unseen book of eternal destiny. This book of human character is not determined by circumstances or time. It is determined by the degree of our discipleship. Not those who call, "Lord, Lord!" can be certain of having their names entered there [see Matthew 7:21].

It is salutary to remember that there is a more sinister census-book which is not mentioned, it is only suggested. A book of life has as its necessary corollary, the book of death. Our cheerful, optimistic Christianity which sentimentalizes God to the blurring of moral distinctions could do with a breath of Dr. Johnson's[2] gusty conversation. Boswell[3] records that he silenced triviality by the remark, "I remember that my maker has said that he will place the sheep on his right hand and the goats on his left" [see Matthew 25:33].

It would perhaps be counted morbid today, but there was sanity in Philip of Macedonia's desire for a constant reminder of death. Philip had a slave to whom he gave a standing order. The man was to come in to the king every morning of his life, no matter what the king was doing, and to say to him in a loud voice, "Philip, remember that you must die."

---

2. Samuel Johnson ("Dr. Johnson," 1709–1784) was a distinguished English writer, poet, literary critic, etc.

3. James Boswell (1740–1795) was a lawyer and author born in Scotland and famous for his *Life of Samuel Johnson*, published in 1791.

How Far Down Dare I Drink?

Death is the one certainty in our human life and it has been called the "sacrament of sin," because it shows effectively that opportunities have gone forever. At death, life speaks the last word. The life-long drama of the soul reaches a climax which is inevitable, inescapable, unrehearsable, and final. Everything constituting life's record is seen to be unalterable, indelible, and irremediable. It is the closure of human development.

And we shall be judged not by our ideals, our promises, or our professions, but by our achievements, our performances, and our practices. If the first census vies for income-tax; the second might be called a census of outcome tax. Everything must be judged by its end, not by its beginning. The block of marble finds its meaning in the statue; the alphabet achieves its end in the literary sentence; the steel in the finished knife, and the man in the character.

Your life is being lived between two census-books: the registrar's and the heavenly recorder's. Other census-books are also being compiled: books of honor, books of privilege, and books of fame. Would you rather be written down in them, than in the lamb's book of life? Would you rather be a patriotic citizen of the British empire or a faithful citizen? Would you rather be written down as a successful man or woman and win a begrudged half-column in the *Times* obituary notices, or would you rather achieve the immortality of the saints? You will have to make the choice many times. You must decide which counts more for you: the world's well-done, or Christ's, "Enter thou into the joy of thy Lord" [Matthew 25:21, 23].

We are keeping Christmas again. It brings a message incredible by the world's judgments. It tells of the world's failure and of spiritual success, that the incarnate God was a baby in a Bethlehem stable, a carpenter in Nazareth, a nameless Galilean preacher, a suffering man upon a gibbet surrounded by thieves on either side. Truly the foolishness of God is greater than the wisdom of men and the weak things of God put to shame the proud man's boasted strength [see 1 Corinthians 1:25]. The Christian is called to faith, not to success. The first is essential, the second is accidental.

A Christian preacher can give no sounder advice, no more heart-filling consolation than to say, "Look to the end." For that redeems man from worldly anxiety and promises him not the utopia of men, but the communion of God, where in his eternal presence, there is fullness of joy for all.

As I close, let me read to you from *The Pi1grim's Progress*, 1678, a most apposite quotation in a Baptist Church:

The Two Census Books

I saw also that Interpreter took Christian again by the hand and led him into a pleasant place where was built a stately palace; at the sight of which Christian was greatly delighted. He saw also upon the top thereof certain persons walked who were clothed in gold. Then said Christian, "MAY WE GO IN THITHER?" Then the interpreter took him in. There also sat a man at a little distance from the door, at a tableside, with a book and an inkhorn before him, to take the name of him that would enter therein. He also saw that in the doorway stood many men in armor to keep it, being resolved to do the man that would enter what hurt and mischief they could. Now was Christian somewhat in a muse: at last when every man started back for fear of the armed men, Christian saw a man of a very stout countenance come up to the man that sat there to write, saying: "Set down my name, Sir." The which, when he had done, he saw the man draw his sword and put a helmet on his head and rush toward the door upon the armed men, who laid upon him with deadly force; but the man not at all discouraged, fell to cutting and hacking most fiercely; so after he had received and given many wounds to those that attempted to keep him out, he cut his way through them all, and pressed forward into the palace, at which there was a pleasant voice heard from those that were therein, "Come in, come in, eternal glory thou shalt win." So he went and was clothed with such garments as they. Then Christian smiled and said, "I think verily I know the meaning of this."

I wonder . . . Do you?

RESPONSIBILITY

Communion Address
Glorifying in the Cross
God Is a Player
May 5th, 1946

> Jesus said to them, "Are ye able to drink the cup that I drink?"... They replied, "We are able." (Matthew 20:22; Mark 10:38–39)

Our Savior was making his way through tragedy to triumph, going up to Jerusalem with palms: Jerusalem with Gethsemane's moonlit garden and deepening shadows... Jerusalem with its ironic crown of thorns... Jerusalem with its open sepulcher. And with that gallant sacrifice and glorious resurrection in mind, the two fishermen interrupted his meditations with a trivial and an absurd question.

They said in effect, "When you're king, we want to share your power and glory, one of us on your right and the other on your left." And our Lord gives them a question in reply, "Are you able to drink the cup that I drink?" Can they drink the cup of disappointment, the cup of suffering, the cup of death and desolation to the very bitter dregs? "Are you worthy of the triumph of the Son of God?" And the foolish fishermen answered, "We are able... Of course, we can!" They were no more foolish than Peter who swore that even if everyone denied the Easter, he would be true, and would prove it with his life. They were no more foolish than you and I are, with our Christian protestations and our unchristian failures.

I want us to look at the master's question more than at the disciples' answer. The dire question is more important than the human assertions, "Are you able to drink the cup that I drink?" Our beloved Lord and king puts that question to every soul gathered in his name here. In this question, we see the inspiration of the gospel. The point is that he who asks for loyalty proves his loyalty by drinking of the cup. The Christ who calls for the red wine of sacrifice to be spilled is the first to break the chalice of his own body that his blood may flow for the healing of the world. All that and more is meant by the cup that he drinks, "This cup is the new testament in my blood" [Matthew 26:28; Mark 14:24; Luke 22:20; 1 Corinthians 11:25]. The wine is the rich red wine of life; the blood is the most [precious] blood of Christ.

If the Christian, burdened by the weight of his difficulties, his sorrows, his disappointments, is tempted to cry, "What right have you, O Christ, to demand this sacrifice from me?" the answer is, "This cup... By these holy wounds in my side, by the crown of thorns... By these nail-prints in my hands; these are my claims to your devotion."

You and I are perpetually amazed by the mysteries of God's providence; more than amazed, sometimes deeply perplexed. Seeing the innocent suffer, and the splendidly promising cut down in their youth; for a moment the sunshine gleaming from heaven and eternity is clouded over by the injustice of the present. In these dark seasons of the soul, when we have forgotten the resurrection of our Lord, and the fullness of life that waits beyond, we are tempted to feel that life is an unrelieved tragedy; that this blow has hit us and hit us only, and God cannot care. We cry, with Thomas Hardy, as he sees his heroine Tess wrongly hanged in Winchester prison, "Justice was done and the President of the immortals... had finished his sport with Tess."[1] We would shake our fists in the very face of the maker of the universe, to call him to account for the evil and injustice. But, my friends, Hardy could just as easily have written, "Justice was done and the president of the immortals... had finished his sport with Christ." And that is, with himself.

---

1. Thomas Hardy (1840–1928) was an English novelist and poet. The reference is to *Tess of the d'Urbervilles* (1891).

Communion Address

However unfair this world may be in its rules, the message of the gospel is, in Canon Roger Lloyd's[2] words, "that God freely chose to come into the game of life as a player, to enjoy no single advantage not open to the other players, to abide by the rules of the Game of a life as player, and to take the consequences." The meaning of Christ's life and death is God-with-us, Emmanuel. God in the flesh is crucified on the Cross. He drinks the cup to the bitter sediment.

Christ leads us through no darker rooms than he went through before. He invites us to follow him, not to go before into the darkness. He is the pioneer. And it is that knowledge that reconciles us to God.[3] For God suffered and still suffers in our sufferings. He is touched with the feeling of our iniquities.

II. And the second message of the gospel in this text is a call, "Are you able to drink of my cup?" Are you able to enter into the fellowship of my sufferings? Can you glory in your cross?

2. Canon Roger Lloyd (1901–1966) was an Anglican priest and author.

3. This insight is central to the Christian theology of reconciliation and to Christian faith. As commonly put, this God "takes God's own medicine." "And it is that knowledge that reconciles us to God"—*if* we are reconciled. The recognition that this God is not aloof but is "in the thick of things," that "God is a Player," opens the possibility of our falling in love with and marveling in the glory of this odd God. All reconciliation, forgiveness, atonement, is mutual, two-way. But Paul gets the "directionality" of reconciliation right: "All this is from God, who through Christ reconciled us to himself ... God was in Christ reconciling the world to himself ..." (2 Corinthians 5:18–19). Consistently for Paul the direction of reconciliation is from us to God ("us to himself," "world to himself"), not because God's reconciliation to us is not essential but because it is "always already." Karl Barth (1886–1968) affirms this vividly in declaring "The Covenant as the Internal Basis of Creation" –*Church Dogmatics*, III, 1, eds, G. W. Bromiley, T. F. Torrance, trans. J. W. Edwards, Rev. O. Bussey, Rev. Harold Knight (Edinburgh: T. & T. Clark, 1958), pp. 228–329. Barth writes, "The fact that the covenant is the goal of creation is not something which is added later to the reality of the creature ..." (p. 231). Again: "If creation was the formal presupposition of the covenant, the latter was the material presupposition of the former" (p. 232). If God were not resolved to see creation through to victory—covenant—there would be no creation. If God were not reconciled to us, there would be no us. We are the reconciliation holdbacks, holdouts. Henri J. M Nouwen (1932–1996) shares Davies's insight: "The real pain is the pain that I find in God, who allowed all of earth's suffering to enter into his divine intimacy"—*The Genesee Diary: Report from a Trappist Monastery* (Garden City, New York: Doubleday & Company, Inc., 1976), p. 121. Hans Küng (1928-) makes the point directly: "Man has to be reconciled, not God. And the reconciliation is entirely due to God's initiative [here Küng references 2 Corinthians 5:18]: what is removed is not God's personal animosity, but that real enmity between man and God ..."—*On Being a Christian*, trans. Edward Quinn (Garden City, New York: Doubleday & Company, Inc., 1976), p. 425.

How Far Down Dare I Drink?

I think we all have them: great crosses, or little crosses. They may be ambitions that had to be given up, laudable or worthy ambitions. I don't suppose there is a man or woman in our church whose life has worked out according to plan, to their plan. Each of you would tell me, as many of you have told me in private, of the frustrations, disappointments, and thwarting of your purposes.

One would speak of an only-child, the most precious treasure in the home, of the dreams the parents had for her; and this little one was called home to God before her fifth year, and the house had crashed. Another would tell of how she gave up all offers of marriage to look after her aging parents. Another tells of how her fiancé was killed at the front, and life seemed to be a bleak winter, with no promise of a second spring. Men tell me of wives, beloved companions of a life-time, and a now empty chair beside the hearth. These only probe wide again the wounds of the heart.

Other men, who have struggled, and worked, and fought to improve their position, and all in the hope to ease the skimping, and scraping that had to be done at home; and no advancement came, no recognition. Others again, looking to the future for quietness and rest after a hard struggle, find the restrictions of life almost too much. They say, and I agree with them, "It's a hard life for old folk today." At only a fraction of the worries, and the disappointments, and bereavements represented in this congregation, to every one of you and your friends, our Lord says, "Take up your cross and follow me" [Matthew 16:24; Mark 8:34; Luke 9:23] and "Are you able to drink of the cup that I drink?" My dear people, do you not see that these things are the testing of your loyalty to Christ? He doesn't ask you to throw the palm at his feet but he asks you to put your lips to the cup of sorrow, and to drink that bitter draught gladly, as you might a toast gallantly, and bravely . . . Are you grumbling or glorying in the cross, in your cross?

To chafe against it is not to conquer it. Acceptance for the sake of Christ is the solution: to offer these slings and arrows of misfortune,[4] to bear them in your body, or in your soul, the marks of the Lord Jesus. These are offerings more precious than the money-gifts you bring, for they have carved their cost into your souls. And what a deep and holy joy this attitude of acceptance brings to life!

Let me take one example that is rarely out of my mind of a man who became great by accepting his cross. The man is President Roosevelt. He

---

4. See William Shakespeare (baptized 1564–1616), *Hamlet, Prince of Denmark* (1599–1602), Act III, i.

Communion Address

was smitten down in his 42nd year with infantile paralysis which crippled him and seemed to put an end to his political career. How could such a man, disabled, face the tumult and hustle of political life? What was left but to retire gracefully from the arena with good grace? But no, he proved there was more than that left to him. He accepted the cross of disability, and made his weakened strength go further than any man. He turned his trouble into a triumph; his weight became wings, his cross, and his crown. His intimates tell us that even when he was resting in his yacht, the one item in the day's business never forgotten was the morning and evening services.

His cross accepted as a challenge did not produce bitterness. No, it produced a sympathy that was an essential part of his greatness, and a courage that enabled him to stand for the truth. The lightning of political opposition was stabbing that great oak of a man to move him from his convictions.

Samuel Rutherford[5] put it thus, "A Cross is such a burden as wings are to a bird, or sails to a ship." It is in the bearing of the crosses that we come to our full spiritual maturity, that we prove our kinship to Christ.

There is a beautiful poem which seems to say all that I have tried to say and to sum it up. It is the story of a soul that shrank from the hard road but finally accepted it, and found happiness unspeakable:

> I said, "Let me walk in the fields,"
> He said, "No, walk in the town,"
> I said, "There are no flowers there,"
> He said, "NO flowers, but a crown."
>
> I said, "But the sky is black;
> There is nothing but noise and din."
> But He wept as He sent me back,
> "There is more," He said, "there is sin."
>
> I said, "But the air is thick,
> And fogs are veiling the sun."
> He answered, "Yet souls are sick,
> And souls in the dark undone."
>
> I said, "I shall miss the light,
> And friends will miss me, they say."

---

5. Samuel Rutherford (c. 1600–1661), Scottish Presbyterian pastor, theologian, and writer.

How Far Down Dare I Drink?

> He answered me, "Choose tonight
> If I am to miss you, or they." . . .
>
> I cast one look at the fields,
> Then set my face to the town;
> He said, "My child, do you yield?
> Will you leave the flowers for the crown?"
>
> Then into His hand went mine,
> And into my heart came He,
> And I walk in a light divine
> The path that I feared to see.[6]

So it always is. And so it may be that when he asks you, "Can you drink the cup I drink?" you shall answer, more quietly than James and John, and more truly, "I can."

---

6. George MacDonald (1824–1905), *What Christ Said*.

The Christian Sense of Direction
A Pilgrimage from God to God

He set his face steadfastly to go to Jerusalem. (Luke 9:51)

I am the way, the truth, and the life ... (John 14:6)

Have you ever been lost? As a child in a maze, when you could find no exit, and all the twisting roads with high neatly clipped hedges seemed exactly alike? As an airman, or a passenger on an airplane, when over the desert or on trackless wastes, without radar? As a yachtsman or in a rowing boat, when the winking lights of the harbor were blanketed by a dense night fog? As an amateur climber, high on a Scottish tor, climbing up scree, with mist behind and before? Or simply as a man or woman, boy or girl, desperately undecided which way to turn when an important decision has to be made, such as career, marriage or adoption? Of course you have been lost. Perhaps you are still lost or at least perplexed and confused. We all need direction. Where are we to find it?

1. In things? Many folk have decided that possessions and accomplishments give direction. What are we working for? An attractive three or four bedroom house, centrally heated, with a garage and tool-shop for the husband, and a shiny kitchen for the wife, with refrigerator, electric-polisher, electric washing and drying, and possibly an automatic dishwasher. A television set and possibly one with ITV adaptation if at present you only have BBC.

I could continue the catalogue indefinitely. If life consists in the abundance of things a man or family possesses, you can obviously always add to them, whether you collect gadgets, or roses, or stamps, or liqueur bottles. But you know as well as I do that while everyone is entitled to the

How Far Down Dare I Drink?

necessities of life, the contented folk are not necessarily well to do. And life can be wasted in getting and spending. I have learnt, in whatever state I am, to be content.

2. In going with the crowd: the cult of conformity? This is the great disease of modern times. It used to be keeping up with the Jones; now it's keeping up with the Armstrong-Jones.

However there are also dangers to the Welfare State. To a certain extent, we are and must be social beings. We are interdependent and the welfare state has been accomplished in part through mass-production and distribution of goods so that not only Lord Nuffield,[1] but also Sam Smith can afford the mini-minor, and Dame Margot Fonteyn[2] as well as Molly Smith can buy St Margaret's woolen vests at Marks and Spencers. The welfare state, by means of socialist and Christian opinion, has ironed out the gross difference between haves and have-nots. I see in it the fulfillment of the biblical warning, "How can I love the God I have not seen, if I do not love the brother I have seen" [see 1 John 4:20].

So far, so good. But I am alarmed that social pressure in monolithic education (comprehensive schools), tabloid newspapers, book-club selections, and television entertainment for the same faceless millions, night after night, should wipe out individuality—the willingness to dare to be different. And I can readily understand the younger generation turning its force against respectability, dull respectability, and saying: "your fox-trot's too slow for me and my gang: we want espresso bongo." It is a protest, an odd protest I grant you, but a real one. It's a vote for cool cats and against sleek domesticated routinized Tabby-cats, all purr and milk. Its error is that it is a social protest, one gang (the young) against the other gang (the middle-aged).

3. In contrast to all this, a third way suggests itself—to go alone—to be utterly different, cranky, eccentric, and odd. I won't waste my life getting possessions; I won't waste my life going with the crowd; I'll be myself. Some have succeeded in this; thousands have failed, and they are to be found in psychiatric wards because they attempted the impossible. Their idea of themselves was so different from their own capacities that their

---

1. William Richard Morris (1877–1963), motors manufacturer and founder of Nuffield College, Oxford.

2. Dame Margot Fonteyn (1919–1991) was an acclaimed English ballerina with The Royal Ballet.

The Christian Sense of Direction

personalities split: the pathetic stunters who lived in a complete dream world, the schizophrenics.

Noel Coward[3] once sent a post-card of the *Venus de Milo* to a small girl and on the back he wrote, "This is what'll happen to you if you go on biting your nails!" This is a parable. To go it absolutely alone is to be lost, to eat oneself away with anxiety and nervous tension.

We can be lost in possessions, lost in a crowd, and lost in the loneliness of ourselves.

How are we to be delivered?

Christ is our deliverer, the shepherd who searches until he finds the lost sheep [see Luke 15:4–7], the ones who have distended stomachs through possessiveness, the ones who have followed the crowd and become caught in the brambles, and the dare-to-be-different ones, lost in the mists. But how? But how?

1. Christ our Lord knew that contentment was found in doing God's will, "A man's life consisteth not in the abundance of a man's possessions" [Luke 12:15]. "Lay for yourselves treasures in heaven where moth and rust do not corrupt and thieves can't break in and steal" [Matthew 6:19; Luke 12:33]. "Foxes have holes and the birds of the air nests, but the son of man hath nowhere to lay his head" [Matthew 8:20; Luke 9:58]. Poverty of possessions freed him for the inches of the spirit. "Brethren," says Paul, "you know that though our Lord Jesus Christ was rich, for your sakes, he became poor, that through his poverty he might become rich" [2 Corinthians 8:9]. Yes in God's will lies our peace—the ultimate destiny for which we were created.

2. He set his face steadfastly to go to Jerusalem [see Luke 9:51]. The crowd! How could we go with the crowd that cried, "Hosanna in the Highest!" [Matthew 21:9; Mark 11:10] when they thought he was the leader of a New Deal, and, "Crucify him!" [Matthew 27:22; Mark 15:13; Luke 23:21] when they preferred a Robin Hood like Barabbas ... The changeling crowd! He knew this; he was the eternal Son of God; and yet he set his face steadfastly to go to Jerusalem, to ugly death and vile dishonor, and to the proving of faith and the ultimate victory of the resurrection.

3. He went alone; the disciples forsook him, and God. Yet he was not ultimately alone. For God and all his saints were with him in the spirit.

---

3. See n. 7, p. 61 above.

How Far Down Dare I Drink?

His gospel has revealed that life is a pilgrimage from God to God, that we must travel light who go so far, and that the happy pilgrims who go with us are the faithful of all the centuries from Abraham to our Christian neighbor. And Jesus is our pioneer, the way, the truth, and the life [see John 14:6].

> Seeing that we have so great a cloud of witnesses . . . let us run the race that is set before us, looking with Jesus, the pioneer and perfecter of our faith, who for the joy that was set before him endured the cross, despising the shame, and is now seated at the right hand of the throne of God. (Hebrews 12:1–2)

Mystery or mysticism? No. Our pilgrims attest that it is the master who alone gives the lost Christian direction in the gospel, in his sacraments, and in the company of his church.

Let us pray:

Merciful master, who willest not that any of thy children should walk in darkness, pour the light of thy spirit into our minds and hearts, that we may know thy will, and, in it, peace for ourselves, and our families, and our world. Let us henceforward walk steadfastly in the paths of heavenly wisdom until we reach thine eternal Jerusalem, to the glory of thy holy name.

Advent
Fulfillment and Finality

> God who at sundry times and in divers manners spake in time past unto the Fathers by the prophets, hath in these last days spoken to us by his son ... (Hebrews 1:1)

If the commodious charabanc is the symbol of the Victorians, the compressed Austin-Seven is the symbol of today. *The Encyclopedia Britannica* has been ousted in favor of *The Reader's Digest*. The seven-course dinner retires in favor of the snack; the ponderous family Bible is set aside for the bedside Bible; the Old Testament is replaced by Moffat's version of the New. This desire for compression, this concentration on the essence, this Bovril for beef, has advantages. If the family Bible was used only as a paper-weight to hold the newspapers in place, then it is better to read the more manageable Moffat in an intelligible tongue. But this desire for compression and brevity has attendant dangers: the Sermon on the Mount is not the whole of the gospel; the New Testament is only understood on the background of the Old.

I turn to my text as a reminder that the New Testament is the fulfillment of the Old. "God who at sundry times and in divers manners spake in time past unto the Fathers by the prophets, hath in these last days spoken to us by his son." The point is that God did speak through the prophets; they were the preparation for the gospel, the patient tilling and fertilizing of the ground in which the seed of the gospel should be planted.

I have recently seen a Russian icon, an altar picture, which illustrated this important truth. The picture is entitled *The King Comes to Zion*. Our Lord is seen making his triumphal entry into Jerusalem; some are cutting down branches from the trees; others are spreading these branches, and their garments on his path. But these are small figures, apparently children. Behind our Savior come the twelve disciples. But another group of bearded patriarchs come to welcome him; they also bear the palm of greeting in their hands. The disciples appear young in comparison with this group of men, whose hair the snow of the ages has whitened. And their garb is centuries out of date. Who are these? They represent the prophets. The prophets enter with him into Jerusalem. They cannot enter until he comes. They have been waiting for his advent. Perhaps the mountain in the background of the picture, with its terraces or flat places, represents the place where the prophets have been standing waiting for him, scanning the distance for the first sign of his coming. This Jesus Christ is the desire of the ages.

An early English hymn has caught perfectly the significance of the prophetic preparation:

> Christ, Desire of Ages,
> Theme of sacred pages,
> Prophesied by sages,
> He my heart engages,
> And my grief assuages.

Imagine the conversation of the prophets who lead the long-expected king into triumph to the city of Jerusalem:

> ONE: This is He whom I saw in the bush in the likeness of fire.
> ANOTHER: This is he that came down amid the crashes and mighty lightening and was heard in the trumpet voice on Sinai's summit.
> ONE: He is the faithful remnant of Israel; this is the stock of Jesse; promised to our Fathers.
> ANOTHER: Shall God indeed dwell with men?
> ANOTHER: Lo! Emmanuel: God-with-us.

They vied in applying to him the names of the long-expected messiah: they called him the day-spring, the morning-star; the shepherd of Israel, the king, a head and counselor, the Lamb, a prince of peace and righteousness; and a strong voice proclaimed, "Make straight the way of our God" [John 1:23; see Isaiah 40:3]. With all these titles he was magnified as he entered Jerusalem, proclaiming the messiahship.

And everyone there knew that this was fulfillment and finality. These are the two themes of Advent that I want to dwell upon.

Advent

Fulfillment

Christ's coming was essentially fulfillment. He is, says Paul, the yea to all the promises of God; the Old Testament foreshadows him, just as the shadow of a man coming round a corner tells you that the man will follow.

We know the importance of this from some words of Jesus to the two disciples on the road to Emmaus. We are told by St. Luke that he said to the benumbed disciples, "O fools and slow of heart to believe all that the prophets have spoken: ought not Christ to have suffered these things and to enter into his glory?" "And beginning at Moses and all the prophets, he expounded unto them in all the Scriptures the things concerning himself" [Luke 24:27]. We are given no hint as to the particular passages the Lord had in mind except the one essential point: that it was necessary for the messiah to suffer.

But we can guess what these were from the very first sermons which the apostles preached in the book of Acts. There their continual theme is that Jesus the messiah was the fulfillment of prophetic hopes and statements.

Here are the points mentioned:

1. God fulfilled his messianic promises:

By sending a word of salvation, as promised in Psalm 117.

By preaching good tidings of peace, as promised in Isaiah 52.

In him, of the seed of Abraham, all the families of the earth might be blessed, as promised in Genesis 22.

Through his church, which he has set for the light of the Gentiles, as promised in Isaiah 49.

2. This promise is fulfilled in Jesus of the seed of David. For he was like David, a man after God's own heart, to whom God promised that he would set upon it Israel's throne of the fruit of his loins, as promised in 2 Samuel 7.

3. Who Jesus is.

Jesus is the Lord's messiah foretold in Psalm 2.

He is the prophet like Moses to whom the people were solemnly told to listen, as mentioned in Deuteronomy 18.

He is the Servant of the Lord, prophesized in Isaiah 42.

4. His Crucifixion.

He was led as a sheep to the slaughter; he was dumb as a lamb before his shearer, as Isaiah 53 predicted.

Against him the Gentiles raged and the rulers were gathered together, as Psalm 2 prophesized.

How Far Down Dare I Drink?

They pronounced him accursed, hanging him upon a tree, as foretold in Deuteronomy 21.

5. His resurrection.

But God did not suffer his holy one to see corruption, as Psalm 16 promised.

God made the stone which the builders rejected the headstone of the corner, as Psalm 118 predicted.

6. His ascension.

God has made him to sit at his right hand, as Psalm 110 prophesized.

7. From him has come the outpouring of the spirit of the Lord.

The messianic gift of spirit is poured out on all flesh, as Joel foretold.

The conclusion of the preaching was in the warning of Habakkuk, "Beware lest ye despise the gospel-message: for this is the work of God."

I have given you this long series of citations from the earliest sermons ever preached, to show you that Jesus was the fulfillment of prophetic dreams, a blessed hope become real and actual.

He was the fulfillment of God's promises. It is for this reason that the Old Testament was the Bible of the early church and that it should be read today. It is in sober truth the cradle of Christ. He was born in the aspirations of the prophets before he was born in Bethlehem. At this time of Advent, we give God thanks for the patience of his preparation of the gospel, and we marvel at the hope of the prophets which burned like a candle amidst the despondency and despair of their times. I bid you consider the amazing providence of God in the Old Testament. Note that in him is the "yes," the confirmation of all God's promises. The prophets had not seen, yet they believed.

We must strengthen our faith putting ourselves in their position. And like them, we have not seen, but yet must believe.

> Jesus these eyes have never seen
> That radiant form of thine
> Yet though I have not seen and still
> Must rest in faith alone;
> I love thee, dearest Lord, and will
> Unseen but not unknown.[1]

Like the prophets, we walk not by sight, but by faith.

---

1. Ray Palmer (1808–1887) was a Congregational minister and writer in New England.

Finality

But unlike them, we know the finality of Jesus. He has come, the Savior promised long. We know not only God's promises, which are all they had, but God's fulfillment. We are no longer men and women seeking in every demagogue a leader, a messiah. We know that Jesus Christ speaks the final authoritative word of God. He is, quite literally, the last Word, "God hath in these last days spoken to us in his son" [Hebrews 1:2]. These words breathe certainty and finality. St. Peter echoes the sentiment they express by saying, "There is none other name given under heaven whereby we must be saved" [Acts 4:12].

And that assurance has made men, through the Christian centuries, into martyrs, missionaries, teachers, inspiring them to undertake the herculean task of saving the world, not by guess, but by God. That is what has made Christians people in a hurry, while others may debate with the leisure of philosophers. Christians have got on with the job. They have received a commission, a divine imperative, and a summons from God.

The Christian does not ask John the Baptist the question, "Art thou he that should come or look we for another?" [Matthew 11:3; Luke 7:19–20]. The Christian knows.

> Finding, following, keeping, struggling,
> Is he sure to bless?
> Saints, apostles, prophets, martyrs
> Answer "Yes."

Burning Bushes and Blackberries
Giving, Getting, and Different Pairs of Eyes
A Youth Sermon

And Moses said, "I will turn aside and see this great sight, why the bush is not burnt." (Exodus 3:3)

[God] said, "But I will be with you; and this shall be the sign for you, that I have sent you: when you have brought forth the people out of Egypt, you shall serve God upon this mountain." (Exodus 3:12)

Are boys interested in trees? I needn't ask the question. Of course you are . . . In many different kinds of trees. You scouts know a lot about trees. Ash trees? What do you do with them? You make scout poles out of them.

Dead wood? What do you do with that? Of course you make fires with it and cook sausages on the burning twigs, until sometimes you cannot tell which is the sausage and which is the twig. And sometimes you cook Irish stew on them—stuff you wouldn't eat if mother put it on the table. But, if you've cooked it, then you swallow hard, and pretend it is a dish fit for a king.

You make model-boats out of trees, and gliders too. You tear your clothes on trees. You make fires out of dead trees; you make bivouacs from them when you are camping. Of course, you are interested in trees.

I don't think girls are quite as interested in trees, although some girls can climb up a tree like a cat. But who knows a girl who does not like decorating a Christmas tree?

Burning Bushes and Blackberries

Boys and girls are interested in trees. So is the Bible. God's book has a lot in it about trees, and smaller trees—or bushes. What were the trees that the poor Jews wept under, when they were taken into captivity? ... Willows [see Psalm 137:1–2]. What was the tallest tree in Palestine—the tree that Solomon used to build the magnificent Temple with [see 1 Kings 6:9]? What was the tree that little Zachariah climbed up on? You know, the one that he hid in and peeped at Jesus through the branches? A sycamore [see Luke 19:4].

I want to tell you a story about a very small tree. It was really just a bush. I want you to know what happened to a shepherd at this bush.

He set out early in the morning, about six o'clock, just the time when you are snoozing peacefully, and the first rays of light were shooting through the sky like a handful of God's torches. His clever little dog was in front of him, running round and round the sheep, like a sergeant major keeping the sheep in good order. He was barking and said in doggie-language, "Left-right; bow-wow, left-right."

The shepherd was a young man, straight of limb, strong of shoulder and with muscles like steel. He carried a staff in his right hand and something like a haversack over his back, to keep his wheat-cakes and oil in and a flask to carry his water. The shepherd, the dog and the sheep walked for many miles through very dry country, like a desert. They couldn't stop there because there was no grass for the sheep to eat. You could have told how hot and dry they were by watching the dog's tongue. He was breathing very heavily, just like that ... (Noise of dog breathing)

The sheep, I expect, were thinking sheepish thoughts. They were dreaming of meadows, full of lush, juicy grass. The dog was thinking, "What stupid nuisances these sheep are. They've no sense at all, or they wouldn't be wanting to lie down here where there's no grass. And they wouldn't be wasting my time by running about in every direction. Really, this isn't a dog's life. Silly sheep! Still, what's the use of grumbling? I shall have a nice fat bone to chew on, when I get home tonight." And as he thought of that, his eyes twinkled, and he licked his chops.

The shepherd, now, what was he thinking about during the long journey? I'm sure he didn't notice the long miles he was trudging, and he had completely forgotten about the sheep. He was thinking very long and very deep thoughts.

He was not thinking of beautiful things, but of ugly things. He was remembering the rest of the clan at home. He had escaped from it all ...

from it all; but the people at home were suffering. He thought of them and he shuddered as he saw them—some of them very old men and young women—carrying huge stones on their backs, to make a great palace for the king of Egypt. He saw them staggering under their heavy loads, with bent backs and red, bruised hands. And worst of all, he could see them wince with pain as the Egyptian foreman whipped them. When he returned home, they used to show him the weals on their arms, and the blue stripes on their backs where the Egyptians had lashed them. And he said quietly to himself, "O God, you were the God of my fathers, and they trusted you. Please help us now. We must get out of Egypt and only you can show us how. O God you must help us." He tried to think of every possible way of freeing the Jews from being the slaves of the Egyptians.

While he was thinking, the dog gave a great yelp of delight. The shepherd looked up and in the distance; there was a valley and a hill. It was now midday, and the sun was blazing down directly above them. So he told the dog to hurry and he made the sheep run faster until they came to the hill. And they all rested in the shelter of the hill. The dog and the sheep slaked their thirst at the cool hillside stream. And the sheep merrily munched the grass. But the shepherd went on thinking.

Suddenly he looked up and saw a bush on the hillside above him, a bush that was blazing with light. It was golden with flames. He had never seen anything like it before. It seemed as if it was burning, and yet, the bush did not burn out.[1] Perhaps anyone else might only have seen a bush with the sun shining on it; but to the shepherd, it was a sign that God was there.

Immediately he saw it, he did two strange things. He took his sandals off his feet and he hid his face. They were signs of reverence. He seemed to hear God saying to him, "Moses, Moses," and he answered, "Here I am, Lord" [Exodus 3:4]. And God seemed to say to him, "Take your shoes off your feet, for this place is holy ground" [Exodus 3:5]. And so Moses, the shepherd, knelt on the ground because he was in the presence of God; as you kneel beside your bed at night, in the presence of God.

While he knelt there, God said to him, "I know the sadness of my people in Egypt; I have heard them cry as their taskmasters whipped them; I am going to set them free from the Egyptians and bring them to a happier land. I am going to send you, Moses, to the king of Egypt and you shall set them free" [see Exodus 3:7–10].

---

1. A striking image of how the biblical God can show up in the world without showing the world up.

Burning Bushes and Blackberries

The shepherd was surprised and shocked "But," he said to God, "how can I do that? I am an exile. I am not even allowed in Egypt and I don't deserve the honor of bringing them out of slavery. I am a nobody" [see Exodus 3:11]. And in the quietness, God answered him, "You are not going alone. I am going with you. You can count on that. You have discovered me here in the burning bush. And I promise you that you shall bring your people here to this place to give me thanks and worship me" [see Exodus 3:12].

Moses found God present in the burning bush. God called him to a great task; God promised to help Moses. And you bet that he kept his promise.

God calls other people too. But they don't hear or they won't listen to him. As Mrs. Elizabeth Barrett Browning wrote:

> Earth's crammed with heaven
> And every common bush afire with God,
> But only he, who sees, takes off his shoes,
> The rest sit around and pick blackberries.[2]

Mrs. Browning helps us to understand in those lines that there were burning bushes and blackberries. Now blackberries are lovely things. It isn't wrong for us to keep our eyes on them and look out for the finest things we can get in the world, for other people as well as for ourselves. But a bush cannot be both a blackberry and a burning bush at the same time.

When you have your eyes open for blackberry bushes, you are looking out for something you can get; when you are on the lookout for burning bushes, you must be ready to give something. That means really a different frame of mind, a different outlook. If you like, you need, in a way, different pairs of eyes.

To look at a burning bush means that you must give up something. To see only the blackberry bush means you are out to grab something.

Your burning bushes will be different from the one of Moses the shepherd. The bush is the call. Your burning bush may be a friend who, in talking to you, tells you of something fine you might do for the world. Dr. Albert Schweitzer's[3] burning bush was the advertisement to go to Af-

---

2. Elizabeth Barrett Browning (1806–1861), *Aurora Leigh: A Poem in Nine Books* in *The Complete Works of Elizabeth Barrett Browning*, eds. Charlotte Porter and Helen A. Clarke (New York: Thomas Y. Crowell & Company Publishers, 1900), vol. V, p. 110, lines 821–824.

3. See n. 5, p. 60 above.

rica in the missionary magazine. To anyone else, just looking out for good money, it would have been a very common bush.

Your burning bush may be the job you are going to do. If you can see in that job a way of helping men and women—no matter whether you are going to be an engineer, or a builder, an engine-driver, or a nurse—then, that bush is a burning bush.

But when you see the burning bush, you must do what Moses did. You must kneel in the presence of God. You must let him help you. If you don't feel that you can ask God to help you, then, it isn't a burning bush. It's only a blackberry.

If it is a burning bush, then you can be sure that God will say to you, "Certainly I will be with you."

The Cloister, and the Hearth, and the Community[1]

How Far Down Dare I Drink?

Connecticut College Baccalaureate Service

And the Lord answered, "Behold he hath hidden himself in the baggage."
(1 Samuel 10:22)

But Martha was distracted with much serving. (Luke 10:40)

For all of us, [graduating class], parents, and friends ... trustees, administration, and faculty, this is a time of gratitude and of questioning, of looking thankfully backwards, and anxiously forwards.

As you look back over the past four years, it is something to be able to say, "I have survived." Some of you who have only just survived may feel as if you are about to be released from prison. But in fact, a prison and a college are about as opposed as any two institutions could be; for it is easy to get into prison and hard to get out; whereas it is very hard to get into a good college, and only too easy to flunk out. Never have the distracting influences exerted a stronger pull to drag you out of the cloister than is a college: the call to fight to desegregate our nation; the call to enlist in the Peace Corps or in the Marine Corps; and not least, the mating call. You, graduands, have suffered and survived everything from maleness to mononucleosis; from the breaking up of old prejudices and cherished convictions, to learning

---

1. A version of this address is published in *Preaching to a World in Crisis*, "Protests, Profound, and Trivial: A Baccalaureate Address Given at Lehigh University, June 11, 1967," pp. 168–174.

How Far Down Dare I Drink?

that who[ever was] a big fish in a small pool is only a sardine in the world of scholarship. But you leave more mature . . .

It is something also for your parents to say, "We have survived." For you a private education is a privilege; for many of your parents it has meant sacrifices, and in some cases, near penury. You will not know until you become a parent yourself what they have gone without, and gladly gone without. They have refused to be hurt by your casualness, by your assumption that their home was a free hotel for undergraduate transients at a moment's notice, and by your assumption that your parents were as old-fashioned as a gargoyle on a medieval cathedral. Most of all, they have survived your escape into independence. And both they and you are grateful today.

It is, and I speak as a faculty member of a sister institution, also something for your teachers and administrators to be able to say, "We have survived." Reading examination scripts can be a very disillusioning experience. Personally I find grading tolerable for two reasons. The first is that I am always on the lookout for happy howlers, or blessed boners. Even in the dross of the most uninspired papers I look for the glint of fool's gold. A very short time ago a new one was added to the growing crop, and this was the gift of a conscientious student. Everyone at Lehigh University naturally knows that Protestantism began when Martin Luther, professor of theology in the University of Wittenberg and an Augustinian monk, nailed a list of 95 brief topics for discussion on the door of the castle church, which he was ready to argue with the papal envoy selling indulgences. The new slant that I received on the prodigious learning of Martin Luther was this, "The Reformation began in 1517, when Professor Luther nailed 95 PhD. theses on the door of the Castle Church in Wittenberg."

The other consolation in the degrading art of grading is the surprises that late developers, and those who suddenly come alight from within, spring upon their teachers. And I never fail to be delighted by those students who progress from being excited by spell-binders and super-anecdotists, whom they think such fun in their freshman year, to an appreciation for those quieter teachers who have a deep dedication to high standards of scholarship and integrity, and whom the student meets in his upper class years. It is part of undergraduate mythology to think of the faculty as the enemy, and the students as the victims. I doubt if any one of you is more disappointed than a conscientious faculty member when you give less than your best. So, the faculty, too, can say as they have watched your zigzag progression towards knowledge and mental and moral maturity, "We too have survived."

Your Future

But my real concern and yours is for the future. So, in the midst of our joy and gratitude to God in this academic community for your attainments, I want you to face the future as I put some serious questions to you. And here I get to my monitory Scriptural texts. Though they come from two different Testaments, they have one thing in common. They deal with two people, each of whom had splendid privileges, who failed to rise to their moment of responsibility.

Of Saul, whom Samuel had anointed to be the first king of Israel and who was about to be solemnly introduced to his people, 1 Samuel 10:22 records, "And the Lord answered, 'Behold he hath hidden himself among the baggage.'" This great vertical creature who stood a head and shoulder above the others, made himself horizontal and supine, and hid himself among the baggage—lost in the impedimenta of life; an escapist in a time of national crisis and challenge—a mere chameleon, fading into the background. It is as if a king should choose to be a baggage-boy, or as if a college graduate from Connecticut said: "A counter-clerk's job is good enough for me," or, "I am the domestic Tabby-cat type, I can't seem to get interested in community affairs." The other text is taken from Luke 10:40, and it also records irresponsibility on the part of a woman who had unusual opportunities to develop her religious and moral insights, but allowed herself to be entirely absorbed in the routine of domestic duties. She was Martha, who, with her sister Mary and her brother Lazarus, had the inestimable privilege of providing a temporary home for Jesus of Nazareth. This man who lived utterly for others, when he was tired and exhausted by teaching, and healing, and advising, would escape for a brief intermission in their home before the needs of the world called him forth again. Martha loved Jesus, as her sister Mary did, and gave him the devotion of hands that cleaned, and cooked, and tidied. But—this is the point—she did not give him, the great teacher, the devotion of her mind. So it was said sadly of her, "But Martha was distracted with much serving."

Saul's failing was that he did not rise to a time of greatness, to a sense of community responsibility. Martha's failing was that, in a time when the

How Far Down Dare I Drink?

values of civilization were at stake, she failed to meet her responsibility as a transmitter of spiritual and moral values.

I would be bold enough to say that the real test of your education is two-fold; whether in the years that lie ahead your sense of responsibility to the community is sharpened, and your loyalty to the great spiritual and moral values on which civilization depends are deepened. And neither your popularity in the country club, nor your status-symbols (whether they be Post-Impressionist originals, or antiques, or a house with a three-car garage) are any index of whether you are educated morally, or intellectually, or whether you are civilized.

As you leave the cloister for the hearth (or better, for the heart and the career), I want to plead that you remain sensitive to the demands of the cloister and the community, the college and the nation.

If you become submerged in suburbia, then you will feel all too soon the emptiness of the waste land; with T. S. Eliot you will wearily confess, "I have measured out my life with coffee spoons."[2] If you become submerged in wifely and motherly duties, this too can become a weariness of the flesh, and you may as well write your epitaph at the age of forty, "My life is as desiccated as dried diapers."

Thus far, you may be reflecting, "Betty Friedan has mesmerized our speaker with the thesis that the feminine mystique is a misery." No, I dissent from much in that lively book on the role of the modern college woman.[3] I think Betty Friedan greatly underestimates the contribution the married woman makes to the future through the education of her children—it is she, rather than the commuting husband, who is the bearer of civilization's values. She is the transmitter of intelligent curiosity, of tolerance, of sympathy, of compassion, of integrity, and of religious loyalty. I think Mrs. Friedan also gravely underestimates the contribution that local voluntary societies make to the vigor and humanity of our American way of life: from the much maligned P.T.A.s to hospital fetes, from recorders' groups to civic reforming groups. All the same, Betty Friedan is, in my view, entirely right in claiming that the entire purpose of women's education is not fulfilled in domesticity. I think she is right in delineating three stages in the history of the education of women: first, the feminist stage when the pioneers of female education gave women man's education to prove that almost

2. T. S. Eliot, "The Love Song of J. Alfred Prufrock," *The Complete Poems and Plays: 1909–1950.* (New York: Harcourt, Brace & World, Inc., 1952), p. 5.

3. Betty Friedan (1921–2006), *The Feminine Mystique* (1963).

everything a man could do, a woman could do better. The second stage was the more recent feminine mystique stage, when education seemed directed at producing frowsier *hausfraus*. The third stage will be when women are educated to be full personalities, playing a role of leadership in the community, fully the equals of men.

If I am right in espousing this view—and I am sure many faculty members will support me in it—then to give up reading and thinking, to give up painting and music, to give up a professional specialty—even if a whole-time career is impossible—to give up a concern for the future of American civilization, and to retire within the home and the social round, would be to throw away most of the fruits of your education. In the future, we shall need more thoughtful and sensitive women, not less. To give up these gains would be, indeed, to hide among the baggage, and to be distracted with too much serving!

The Claims of the Cloister

Our Western Universities, as you know, sprang from medieval monastic communities, and the oldest of them show their lineage architecturally, with their quadrangles, cloisters, and chapels. Thus do they indicate that the purpose of coming to college is meditation?

We come to learn the nature of the universe, and all the sciences are fascinating avenues into that labyrinth. We come to learn about the role of mankind in the universe, the history of the human race, and the achievements of literature, music, and art. We come to learn about the nature and organization of the human communities in politics, economics, and sociology. We come to learn about human inner potentialities and values, through psychology and philosophy. We also come to learn about those ultimate loyalties that are deeper even than patriotism, which we call religious. The devotion to God has proved able to overcome the three great tragedies of human life: that arrogant self-incurvature, as Augustine termed it, that rides roughshod over the rights of others which theologians call sin and sociologists anti-social behavior; the agonies, and sufferings, and disappointments which all flesh is heir to; and the final threat of death itself. For the threatening world into which you are to be let loose, there is no question that you are going to need the inspiration of faith and the ethical directions that our great Judeo-Christian tradition brings. Reason will, of course, take you far; but, as the poet Watts[4] said:

> Where reason fails with all her powers,
> There faith prevails and love adores.

So I am begging you to take the inspiration of the cloister, intellectual, aesthetic, and religious into your home and your career.

The Claim of the Community.

You have lived in this island-community for four years, but now you move out into the mainland and metropolis of life. You must move out with confidence and courage because your intelligence and your faith are needed. This is the day of challenge and of opportunity.

But the bugle-call of opportunity may be muffled by the false cries of "safety-first," whether they be religious, domestic, or careerist. You will be tempted to think it superior and aristocratic to live with only a balcony view of life, above the political struggles for power, above the slums where your brothers, and sisters, and mine live. But this is a miserable rationalization; it is poor religion and putrid humanity.

Both Jewish prophets and Christian seers warn us that the heart of the law and the prophets is to love God with all our heart, our mind, and our will; and our neighbor as ourself [see Matthew 22:37, 39; Mark 12:30–31; Luke 10:27].

An isolationist religion is a hollow sham, and a mockery. "How can you love the God you have not seen, if you do not love the neighbor you have seen?" [see 1 John 4:20]. The Attorney-General, speaking at a recent exhibition of memorabilia of John F. Kennedy, reminded us that the late President's favorite saying was this, "The hottest places in hell are reserved for those who in times of moral crisis preserved their neutrality."

It is truer today than when Abraham Lincoln first spoke the words, "A nation cannot survive half-slave and half-free." Gunnar Myrdal[5] in his brilliant analysis of *An American Dilemma*[6] pointed out that the American democratic experiment was founded on the belief that all men were

---

4. Isaac Watts (1674–1748), "We Give Immortal Praise" (hymn).

5. Karl Gunnar Myrdal (1898–1987) was a Swedish recipient of the Nobel Memorial Prize in Economic Sciences together with Friedrich Hayek in 1974.

6. *An American Dilemma: The Negro Problem and Modern Democracy* (1944).

The Cloister, and the Hearth, and the Community

free, and all shared in the image of God. Politically and religiously we are committed to that view. That is why millions have sought these shores, attracted by the gleams of freedom's holy light. But, as Dr. Myrdal saw, we have now reached the cross-roads. We can no longer afford the great gap of hypocrisy between our inherited political and religious values, on the one hand, and the maintenance of segregation, on the other hand. Either we must—which, God forbid—change our democratic form of government for a dictatorship of the whites, keeping under all who are black, or brown, or yellow as slaves; and we must openly declare that we worship a white tribal deity; OR, we must live by the religious and political imperatives which we claim to believe in, and live in color-blindness. This is the challenge of today, and I hope you will be in the thick of it to create an America that is again the home of the free.

For six years I lived in a country whose racial problems are more acute than our own, a country that was then ironically called the Union of South Africa. I can recall a simple but moving story which I was told by a social worker. It is a parable. A pathetically poor and hungry African girl came to the welfare office and was offered a glass of milk. Before she allowed it to touch her lips, she glanced across at her younger brother, and she asked, "How far down may I drink?" She might not have been cultured, but she was civilized. And you, each of you, who holds at this moment, in your delicate hands, a Venetian glass with the wine of culture and intelligence glistening at its brim, must constantly ask, as you remember the parched lips of God's underprivileged ones, "How far down dare I drink?"

GRATITUDE

Harvest Thanksgiving
Gratitude

God left not himself without witness in that he did good, and gave you from heaven rain and fruitful seasons, filling your hearts with food and gladness. (Acts 14:17)

St. Paul, because he was a great preacher had the art of adapting himself to his hearers. When he was at Athens facing a scholarly audience, he preached a learned sermon about the purposes of God. When he was at Corinth, the great commercial center, where men were mainly concerned with making money, he determined to speak of nothing "save Jesus Christ and him crucified" [1 Corinthians 2:2] to remind them of the vanity of earthly things. Our text was addressed to a very different audience, the simple, unlettered people of Lystra—people so ignorant that they took Paul and Barnabas for gods. So St. Paul chooses as his subject the simplest of all religious themes, the gratitude we owe to God for rains and fruitful seasons, for food and gladness.

We are all better for being reminded of the gratitude we owe; indeed, it is often the only way to prevent our churlish dissatisfaction with life. None of us can afford to smile at a Harvest Thanksgiving as merely Christian cupboard love. This is not all the faith, but it is the beginning. So we need not call it pagan survival.

How, I wonder, did Harvest Thanksgiving originate in this country? When our Saxon ancestors first invaded this country, they brought with them the custom of sacred feasting and drinking accompanied by the sacrifice of cattle or horses to show their conviction that life was good. Some of the early Christian missionaries were scandalized by such celebrations, but

How Far Down Dare I Drink?

Gregory the Great[1] was wiser. He wrote to the first Bishop of London bidding him that "you cannot cut off everything at once from rough natures. He who would climb to a height must ascend step by step, for he cannot jump the whole way." And so, under his guidance, the heathen feasts were, by degrees, converted into church feasts and harvest festivals.

These words of Gregory's suggest the right attitude to harvest celebrations. Some would condemn them outright as pagan festivals and (very reasonably) complain that they are attended by larger congregations than the greater festivals of the church. If this is true, it shows that the congregation concerned is still in an elementary stage of religious life. But no wise man despises the day of small things, or will fail to see how much good there is in a simple service of gratitude to God, the maker and giver of all good things.

If I may remind you again of the early history of the Christian faith in the north of England, I should like to tell you how the first missionary sent from Iona to Northumbria returned disheartened by the rude manners of the Northumbrian people, saying it was useless "to attempt to convert such people as they are." A monk among those to whom he made his report asked whether he had not perhaps been expecting too much and too soon: had not the Apostle said that milk, not meat, was the food for babes. All eyes were turned on the questioner, and all said simultaneously that he was the right man to undertake the work. So it was that St. Aidan[2] came to Lindisfarne. He found in the simple nature of the Northumbrian people, a foundation on which he could build, and so began one of the most glorious centuries in the history of the church of Christ in England.

We are right to give thanks for the blessings of harvest, but our service will be very imperfect if it stops there. It should lead on to give thanks also for "all the blessings of life," and to remember what those blessings are. We are all in danger of taking them for granted until they are taken away from us. Just as we never remember to be grateful for our health, until we are in danger of losing it; or, to take a simpler instance, to be grateful for our ability to go to sleep until we suffer from insomnia.

What are the blessings which all of us enjoy, the blessings which come to us alone of all created things? First comes our power of appreciating beauty. All of us, at one time or another, have been struck by the beauty of a sunset, bathing the hills in purple and gold. All have seen and wondered

---

1. Gregory the Great, Pope Gregory I (c. 540–604).
2. St. Aidan of (the island of) Lindisfarne (d. 651), Apostle of Northumbria.

Harvest Thanksgiving

at a field glinting with buttercups like a profusion of sovereigns thrown on a green carpet. We have all admired the lonely beauty of the moors, seen gaunt grey rocks softened by the purple delicacy of the heather. We have all seen the changing colors of the trees in autumn, nature's great dress parade, when the mantles of green are laid aside for the variegated browns and golds of autumn. We take our appreciation for granted, but we should do well to remember that it is a place no animal shares. The next time you see a grazing field or your dog running at your side, you might well remember to give thanks that you have a power which is denied to them.

And beauty has many other forms, equally reserved for us alone, as well as the beauty of nature, painting, and architecture, all speak to us and give us a pleasure of their own. And the whole field of literature in drama, story, and poetry, is full of delights, for which we should assuredly give thanks.

And the mention of literature or books leads us on to consider another unique possession of our human race, which is seeking for the truth. We alone of created beings have the power of seeking for the truth. We may not use it wisely or consciously, for we are not all philosophers, but every time that you discuss with your friends any question that interests you, remember that you are exercising a power that belongs to man alone. Whatever your interests may be, it is from God that they come, and you should not fail to give thanks for a power which means so much to the happiness of your life.

Again, an even higher capacity is to understand something of the way in which God works. Every discovery of science is a discovery of his methods, just as every appreciation of beauty means that we are seeing things as God sees them. When the world was made, he saw that it was good [see Genesis 1:25, 31], and we, in our degree, can see with his eyes.

This is even truer when we consider the meaning of our life. The third gift we have been given is the gift of conscience. We were made, as we believe, in the image of God [see Genesis 1:26], and the proof of that lies in the power we all possess in an astonishing degree of knowing the difference between right and wrong. However ignorant or careless we may be, there is none of us who can admire a coward, or a liar, or applaud a selfish action. We are still, as we know to our cost, terribly selfish, and it might be expected that this would give us a prejudice in favor of selfishness. But the exact opposite is the case: we hate selfishness in others; we even hate it in ourselves, however little we may do to conquer it. What clearer proof could there be that we have a divine ancestry? And is not that a reason for thanksgiving?

By the fourth gift of God, we alone of created beings have a true understanding of love. God is love, and here supremely we share in his nature. I do not forget the devotion of the dog to his master—though he may have learned it from his long association with human beings—of the self-sacrifice that other animals show. But love, in its proper sense, is the possession of human beings alone. When we remember how much we owe to our parents and our friends, and how any love we have been able to show lifts our little lives into something higher than their ordinary levels, we shall not fail to give thanks for the greatest of all possessions.

And so we come to the words of the General Thanksgiving, where we give thanks "above all for the redemption of the world by our Lord Jesus Christ, for the means of grace, and for the hope of glory." But that is the subject of other sermons, telling the story of God's love for man, shown in the coming of his son into the world; of what the son did and suffered for our sakes; of his triumph over death, and for the glorious hope which he extends to his followers, not only the blessed hope of everlasting life hereafter, but the opportunity and the power of living here on earth a life which will go on with greater knowledge and with fuller meaning after death.

Today, we have tried to see how the simple acts of thanksgiving for the blessings of harvest lead on to other things. The same God who gave us "rain from heaven and fruitful seasons" [Acts 14:17] has greater things to give: some of them he gave in the mere act of creation; others he will give to those who ask. For he is our Father, and if we, being evil, know how to give good gifts to our children, our heavenly Father will give to those who love and follow him [see Matthew 7:11; Luke 11:13] "good things which pass our understanding."

PART TWO

Cross-Examination
Not from the Comfort of a Pulpit

First Witness
The Mother
Behold the Handmaid of the Lord.

Standing by the cross of Jesus, his mother ... (John 19:25)

I summon Mary as the first witness of the Crucifixion. Look at her carefully, but do not pry too closely. She has borne the weight of fifty tragic years on her slender shoulders. Her hands are worn thin with toil and clasped mechanically in prayer. Her lips are mute, but her stifled sobs speak thoughts that are deeper than tears. Her thin, homespun shabby dress is disarrayed by grief. The beloved disciple has his right arm on her shoulder, but her world is tottering. No hand can arrest its crashing momentum. What are her thoughts?

The sheer futility of the Cross.

It is the immediate natural response of the mother for her son. Her adorable Jesus, whom she had loved as her first and favorite child, was now being extinguished when the flame of his life was at its brightest. She thought of that child so full of promise, whose coming had been foretold by God and the prophets, whom splendid strangers from the East had done homage to in his manger-cradle. She remembered the holy joy of his coming into the world—the head that had nestled at her breast, whose curls she had proudly displayed, and now clotted with gore and pierced with thorns. The bright, eager, and intelligent face that had plied the ponderously learned Pharisees in the Temple with profound questions! "How does that visage languish that once was bright as morn?" She remembered the happy days when Joseph and Jesus came in from the shop to eat the newly-baked bread, the ringing laughter, the quiet moments of prayer, the strange excited way in which he used to read out of the prophets, their dreams for him, and the crowds that used to gather to listen to her son; the pride that welled in her heart, when people whispered in Capernaum, "She's the new prophet's mother." And now look at him! The place was almost empty, the crowds had already forgotten. What did those burly soldiers playing solo at the cross understand? She wanted to take him in her arms again, but he was pinned to the cross. She could not even be alone with him: there were always a few gaping bystanders and the uncouth soldiers. "O God!" she sobbed, "The waste, the waste of it!"

The folly of it.

She never quite understood Jesus. He was always loving and dutiful, a good son; but there was that other side to him that she could never understand. He seemed to join with the other children in his play, but what other child spent whole nights in prayer? Then, she didn't mind the youth setting up as a local preacher, but it was going too far when he criticized the bishops for not doing their duty. And he was asking for trouble that day in Jerusalem, when he actually told the Temple merchants, who had every right to be there, that they were no better than a pack of thieves. Jesus meant well, but he let his tongue run away with him.

She recalled the misunderstandings she had had with Jesus. He was always a little strange. Joseph and she were really frightened when he said to them when he was only twelve, "Why do you worry over me? What is there to be surprised at in my wanting to stay here in my Father's house?" [see Luke 2:49]. It wasn't natural.

Then how harshly he had spoken to her at the wedding at Cana! She was only trying to help, and she knew that he would if he could. "Woman," he said "What have I to do with thee?" [John 2:4]. The words passed like a cold wind over her heart. It seemed like someone else speaking to her.

Then other things that he had said came to her ears. They were very hurtful; they sounded as if he didn't appreciate his mother or his brothers: "A prophet is not without honor, except in his own country, and among his own kindred, and in his own house" [Matthew 13:57; Mark 6:4]. She remembered, too, that under stress, when they thought he was risking his life by his outspokenness, one of his brothers had said, "He is beside himself" [Mark 3:21]. She had to confess that she had often wondered if he was quite normal. But it was his answer that had cut her to the quick. When they told him that his family [members] were in the crowd, he had disowned them. Pointing to the disciples, he said, "Behold my mother and my brethren, for whosoever shall do the will of God, the same is my brother, and sister, and mother" [Matthew 12:49; Mark 3:34–35; Luke 8:21]. But what hurt most of all was what Jesus had said on the triumphant ride into Jerusalem. A woman had cried, "Blessed is the womb that bore thee, and the breasts which thou didst suck" [Luke 11:27–28]. He turned round on her immediately with, "Nay, blessed are they who hear God's Word and keep it" [Luke 11:28].

This she couldn't understand. But then there were many things about Jesus she couldn't understand. He was different. He was famous. He had helped a lot of people. But now he was dying as a common criminal. Why couldn't he have stayed in the carpenter's shop and taken over the business when Josh died? Why, if he had to go, must he attack the official leaders in Jerusalem? It is true that the saintly old Simeon said to her when Jesus was born, "Yea, and a sword shall pierce through thine own heart" [Luke 2:35]. She had not dreamed that he would have struck the sword through her own heart. "O God!" she cried, "The folly, the folly of it!"

These were her beliefs: that the death of her marvelous son was a gigantic waste; and that he had only himself to thank for attacking the authorities. Perhaps, also, there was a third thought that could not find coherent expression.

Perhaps he was right.

Perhaps he was right. But it seemed so much against the facts. He was branded as a blasphemer. But she had never met anyone who knew God as Jesus did. He seemed to know God so much better than he knew even Joseph. Could he be a blasphemer? They said that he claimed to be King of the Jews. But he had refused to be a popular leader, when the crowd asked him to lead them. No. He was never ambitious for himself. Perhaps he was right, and they had all misunderstood him. Her mind flashed back to the scrolls of the prophecies of Isaiah they had at home. One of them was thumbed more than the rest. Jesus was always reading it to them. One day he learned it off by heart. How strange it seemed that her son, sparkling with life, should in those far-off days be reading the saddest of all passages of the Scriptures, "He was despised and rejected of men" [Isaiah 53:3]. That was the passage.

"He is despised and rejected of men." The realization had dawned. Jesus is the suffering servant. He is right. A brilliant dawn two days later was to make the possibility a certainty. But it was more than she dared to hope for.

God has a message to speak to us through Mary at this time. There are a number of Maries and Josephs in this congregation. They are proud that their sons have acted according to their conscience, prouder than they would admit.

But, like this greater Mary, these parents are standing in the shadows of their family crosses. Be honest and confess it. Don't your fears whisper, "O God! The waste of it, the sheer waste of it!" Don't your doubts suggest, "O God! The folly of it!" Don't you sometimes feel that God doesn't care, that you are shouting in the dark and no friendly door opens in the heavens? So did Mary. So also in an agonizing moment did the very Son of God in that cry of dereliction, "My God, my God why hast thou forsaken me?" [Matthew 27:46; Mark 15:34]. You have known that terrible moment when the throne of the universe seems empty, and the world is a dark and impenetrable forest. You are terrifyingly alone, and hear the howling of the wolves of fear.

Fearful and lonely heart, take courage! Like Mary, you will not always understand. But like Mary, you must trust. That was the secret of her endurance: implicit trust.

It is expressed in a peerless sentence when first she knew that she was to bear the messiah, she simply answered, "Behold the handmaid of the Lord; be it unto me according to thy Word" [Luke 1:38].

What is required is obedience from first to last. A modern writer has written, that the incarnation began when Mary said, "Into thy hands I commend my body" and ended when Jesus said, "Into thy hands I commend my spirit" [Luke 23:46; see Psalm 30:5: Jesus knew the psalms]. And obedience has its own divine reward. Those who keep tryst with God through the dark night of trial shall see the clouds of darkness hurrying before chariots of Easter dawn.

Nothing can separate us from the love of God, in Jesus Christ our Lord [see Romans 8:38–39]. Nothing.

Judas Iscariot
Have You Never Met a Judas?

"Judas who betrayed Jesus" [John 18:5]. These four words make the blackest epitaph in history; they commemorate the most dastardly deed ever recorded. Yet they raise two riddles that must be solved. How could Jesus have chosen him as one of his disciples? And how did Judas come to commit the crime?

The choice of Judas.

It seems as if Jesus made a tragic mistake in choosing Judas. The other eleven justified his choice, even if at times they seemed most unsuitable. Thomas the skeptic wouldn't seem to be of much use to a prophet of faith, but he ultimately was convinced. Peter, the blunderer and the denier of Christ, died a martyr. But Judas, he was a thoroughly nasty individual. Sometime before the betrayal, he had been caught red-handed, pilfering the funds of the disciples. As mean and caddish, his betrayal of Christ was on a par with this. He sold his master for thirty pieces of silver, for just over four pounds. Judas, what was he of all people doing in the company of the disciples? A petty pilferer, a deceiver, a scoundrel. Had Jesus a blind-spot in his estimate of human nature when he chose him? Or, was Judas predestined to be the betrayer of Christ, and did Jesus know that all along?

We can rule that out. God does not ordain evil; in his overruling of the universe he permits free will and therefore he allows evil. But he did not will that Judas should betray Christ. Nor did Jesus know, when he selected him, that this man would bring about his death.

Jesus chose him because there were possibilities of greatness in Judas, no more and no less than there were in the rest of the disciples he chose. He must have been a man of great practical ability, or Jesus would never have made him the treasurer of the funds which had to be so carefully eked out to meet their daily necessities, and leave some over for dire cases of poverty. Judas was chosen because he had practical sagacity. He must also have been a man of great enthusiasm—that was the first requisite Christ demanded. He turned the rich young ruler away because he was not whole-heartedly committed to Christ himself. It required enthusiasm of lasting quality to give up all family ties and possessions to follow Christ. That abounding energy and enthusiasm was in Judas, we may be sure. Practical sagacity and enthusiasm are not found round every corner. Judas had the assets and a tremendous opportunity with Jesus.

How then could he bring himself to betray Jesus? What was his motive?

It was only partly greed. A man does not commit the equivalent of murder for four pounds. We know Judas was not scrupulously honest. But no man of his practical wisdom would have been fool enough to risk his own life as well as his sister's death for that price. We must look elsewhere.

It was partly resentment. Can't you see that Judas was the target, when our Lord warned men of the peril of riches? Judas, who always had an eye on the main chance, was addressed in these words, "Lay not up for yourself treasures on earth, where moth and rust consume, and where thieves break in and steal" [Matthew 6:19]. Judas winced at that ugly word, "thieves."

Judas was there, edging away from the front when our Lord spoke of the seed that fell among the thorns, "This is he that heareth the Word; and the care of the world and the deceitfulness of riches choke the Word; and he becometh unfruitful" [Matthew 13:22; Mark 4:19; ; Luke 8:14]. It was to Judas trying to grasp the hand of Christ, and keep the same fingers clasped on the money-box that Jesus said, "Children, how hard it is for them that trust in riches to enter into the kingdom of God. It is easier for a camel to enter the eye of a needle than for rich men to enter the kingdom of God" [Matthew 19:24;; Mark 10:25; Luke 18:25].

The disciples didn't know his weakness, but Jesus saw it, and these shafts of truth were probing the still festering wound in the soul of Judas.

But the largest ingredient was ambition. Remember that Judas was a proud nationalist. He alone of the disciples hailed from Judea: the rest came from Galilee, an unimportant backwash out of the main stream of political life. The Galileans were as uninterested in the national government as a lonely Scottish farmer in Skye, or a Lakeland shepherd out on the Fells. But Judas was a politician.

There is a world of meaning in his surname Iscariot. It has two possible meanings. It may simply mean "man of Kerioth," but Kerioth was a southern district nearer the capital. It was one of the home counties, whilst Galilee was a province in the remote North. But it might mean much more than that. The western Greek text of the Scripture reads "Scariotes" for "Iscariot," and the "Scariots" were a political party of firebrands, known as the Assassins. They were violent partisans of home rule, like the Sinn Feiners of Ireland. Their one aim was to rid Jerusalem of the usurper, and push the Romans into the sea.

If this were the case, it would explain the character and the career of Judas. He joined Jesus because he saw in him the messiah of his hopes. This man braved a mad crowd; he held multitudes spell-bound by his oratory; he could subdue the very winds and waves by his commands; he could raise a dead man to life again. Why! The world lay at his feet, there simply for the asking. Judas couldn't always quite understand him. He was unexpectedly gentle, for one who wielded power. Judas couldn't see why he refused the crown that the people wanted him to take. Sometimes he talked too much about heaven, when heaven on earth was within his grasp. But Judas waited. Yes, he waited, and bore with the insults and the misunderstanding of the master. What did these matter? Soon the day would come when Christ would be the King of the Capital, and Judas his prime minister. Judas could afford to wait.

It looked as if the end that Judas wanted was imminent. Jesus at last had agreed to come up to Jerusalem. He was even going to ride on a donkey to fulfill the prophecies of the messiah. The master talked about suffering. Well he might. Jerusalem couldn't be won without some opposition. Everything was going well. The crowd responded magnificently. There was tremendous applause, cheering, and palm-waving. Judas waited. Only two or three days and his triumph would be complete. They would be in complete control of Jerusalem, and they would march on to rid the coasts of Jewry of these pestilential Romans.

But Judas received the shock of his life. He discovered that Jesus was in Jerusalem to suffer, not in an attack on the capital, but to witness for God the redeeming power of self-sacrifice. The plans would go wrong. Jesus, then, really meant the words, "My kingdom is not of this world" [John

How Far Down Dare I Drink?

18:36]. And as the disappointment grew in his fanatic's eyes, he cried, "By God he shall not fail. He shan't cheat Judea of her deliverance. If I have to force him to perform a miracle, he shall be our national leader."

Like the speed of lightening, the plan matured. He went to the high priests. He knew they wanted Jesus. Very well, let them try to take Jesus. The bargain was made. "I'll tell you where he'll be. After supper he takes a walk in the Garden—Gethsemane, you know." —"But, it will be dark, how shall we know which he is?" they asked. —"If you leave that to me, he'll be the one that I'll embrace." —"How much do you want for this job, Judas?" Judas had almost forgotten that side of things. But he mustn't arouse suspicion: —"Oh, make it the price of freeing a slave. Thirty silver shekels." —"Done." As Judas left them, he murmured, "The fools, the fools. The master will show them."

He had to go through the rest of the evening as normal. He took his usual seat beside Jesus at the supper. "What thou doest, do quickly" [John 13:27], said the master quietly to him. Was that a hint? Did Jesus know? He must put such stupid thoughts behind him. It was his own heated imagination. No time must be lost. Everything went according to plan: soldiers under cover in the trees, high priests lurking behind them, lurking in the longer shadows of the wall. He could hear two disciples in conversation with the master. Now he had left where he was praying. Judas crept nearer. He could hear Jesus sobbing. He couldn't go to him now. He was now calling Peter. This was the hour. He ran to Jesus and kissed him. The moment had arrived. This was Christ's hour of glory. But Jesus did nothing, nothing.

Then something snapped in Judas's brain. He is stupefied. He rushes back to the Temple. He flings the polluted money down. He says, "I have sinned. I have betrayed innocent blood." They answer him, like human icicles, "What do we care?" Judas was helpless. He had set the machine of the crucifixion in progress, and it would move to its ghastly end. And Judas made an end of himself.

There is nothing else to do. A coward's way out? No, it was a pitiable bet of restitution. Judas knew that there was no resurrection for the man who died the death of crucifixion. He believed that he had sent Jesus to eternal doom. He knew, too, that there was no resurrection for suicides. If Christ were to go to hell, then he would live in hell with him. Judas was great in his passing. That alone justified Christ's choice of him.

Judas Iscariot

The Bible does not tell us the circumstances, but John Masefield[1] puts these words into his mouth in the Temple: "Take your silver. I have betrayed that man, but I will be hanged before him; you will find me hanged this day. I will be blasted first, Lord Jesus." A rope and a tree overhanging a precipice, a wild scream, the crack of breaking bones, and Judas made his requital.

There we must leave Judas, the man who betrayed his master because he misunderstood him. The man who tried to force the hand of the king of heaven, because he thought of God's job better than God did.

His failure was due to spiritual pride. And who are we to cast a stone at him [see John 8:7]. Have you never met a Judas? Have you never heard a politician justify his selfishness in the name of God, or of humanity, or of necessity? Have you never heard a Christian grumble that the kingdom of God moves slowly to its climax? Have you, yourself, never cried, "This war is a tragic mistake; O Lord God, stop it!" Have you never tried to serve God and Mammon [see Matthew 6:24; Luke 16:13], to bargain with Annas and Caiaphas, and make your vows to Christ?

Men and women, Judas did not have a leering face, a sinister expression; he was no melodramatic villain with a black beard and a devilish eye. All he had was an internal cancer, and its name was pride.

Turn to the looking glass, and you will find a face not dissimilar to Judas. The face of a good man or a good woman who conceals pride. His betrayal was a climax of little deceptions, small sins, petty peccadilloes, and trivial compromises. Judas is you without Christ.

> O break, O break hard heart of mine!
> Thy weak self-love and guilty pride
> his Pilate and His Judas were:
> Jesus, our Love, is crucified.[2]

Your own mirror is no clue to yourself. Look long and penetrating into the mirror of God, the express image of the Father, Jesus Christ. Then you will find:

> What Christ bids me be,
> He helps me to become.

---

1. See n. 1, p. 39 above.
2. Frederick William Faber (1814–1863), hymn writer and theologian, "O Come and Mourn with Me Awhile."

Caiaphas
Hypocrite as His Soul Deadens

Suppose that you were to pick up tomorrow morning's newspaper and you found this headline splashed across the front page, "Archbishop demands death penalty for preaching." You would think it was an absurd hoax on the part of a practical joker with a poor sense of fun. The whole thing is of course too impossible.

Turn to the gospel, my friends, and you will find that this absurdity is the solemn truth. Archpriest Caiaphas in actual fact demanded that Jesus be put to death for preaching the inviolable truth about himself.

How can we explain the extraordinary fact that the archpriest of the church became its archfiend?

But we must first establish the fact. We have seen already that there is no simple answer to the question, "Who crucified my Lord?" We know that Judas was implicated. He set the machinery of crucifixion in motion. Its initial impetus came from his betrayal of Jesus in the garden of Gethsemane, but it issued in results very different from his intention. We shall see later that Pilate might wash his hands of responsibility, but he could not rub the filth of cowardice off them. If we must fasten on one criminal, it is Caiaphas that we must convict. He is without any possible extenuation the villain of the piece.

It is no exaggeration to say that in cold blood, with careful planning, he was determined to kill Jesus. The plot was a long time hatching, and the devilish subtlety of it was his devising. Judas, Peter, and the penitent thief were all creatures of impulse, hasty and impetuous men. But Caiaphas was more of a viper than a man. And that was the very word which John the Baptist had used to describe these crafty, insincere ecclesiastics. "You generation of vipers," he snarled at them, "flee from the wrath that is to come" [Matthew 3:7; Luke 3:7]. Watch a viper and you will see the portrait of Caiaphas in action. Note its half-hooded, sly eyes, apparently noticing nothing, but alert to every movement in the undergrowth. That was Caiaphas who had spies nosing out any hint of heresy. Note the evasiveness of the viper; see how it glides over every obstacle. So did Caiaphas avoid the enmity of Rome, and retain the approval of his countrymen. Then watch the viper strike its prey; its body is coiled, like a concertina, before it makes the sudden sharp stroke. That was Caiaphas preparing his plans in cold blood, and then striking without an instant's warning. It was this viper, this cold and cynical clergyman, that plotted and executed the death of Jesus.

But why should he wish to destroy Jesus? If we look more carefully at his career we can see that enmity to Jesus was inevitable for him. Two facts make that unmistakably clear. He was a Sadducee, that is, he belonged to the aristocratic party—the upper and only ruling house. He was inevitably a snob who would not take kindly to a carpenter's son setting up as a rabbi and a prophet, and even, so his spies reported, pretending to be the messiah. I can imagine him pooh-poohing the suggestion [that] Jesus was dangerous, when he received the first report, "Do you mean to tell me that this carpenter fellow is going to prove a nuisance? Are you seriously suggesting that I should be worried by this self-appointed messiah and the ragged crowd of halfwits that he has gathered round him? You ought to know your duty better than to bother me with this talk ... Can anything good come out of that poky little Nazareth?" [see John 1:46]. Caiaphas was a snob. He was prejudiced against Jesus from the commencement, even when he had only heard his name mentioned.

Caiaphas was a Sadducee. That meant also that his religion had no love in it. It was a religion of cold and formal obedience to a million precepts. St. Paul, who knew Jewish religion from the inside, was to say of it that it was bondage, a terrifying imprisonment of the personality. And Jesus, in a brief glimpse, painted it in a telling cameo. The priest was the one who saw the casualty on the road to Jericho, plainly saw his gaping wounds, his empty tell-tale purse lying torn on the road; he saw his mute appeal to his humanity, and crossed over [see Luke 10:30–31]. The Sadducee's religion was loveless; it lacked even the common decency of the man in the street. Caiaphas was a priest. And his religion was as distant from the religion of Jesus as the North Pole is from the Equator.

Caiaphas was the high priest of the Sadducees. He had not obtained the office by merit, but by wire pulling. His father-in-law, Annas, had been

How Far Down Dare I Drink?

high priest, was fabulously wealthy, and he used his influence and, no doubt, some of the Temple coinage, to bribe Caiaphas into office.

Jesus and Caiaphas, you will see, were irreconcilable, absolute opposites in temperament, in principles (if Caiaphas had any!). As surely as truth must grapple with error, the conflict was inevitable.

At first, as I have suggested, Caiaphas probably did not condescend to notice the messages of his spies. But before long, he had to take notice. The fame of Jesus of Nazareth was spreading. His teaching was amazingly successful; even Caiaphas's trained hecklers could not trip him up. It was reported that he had actually brought a man back from the grave, a few miles out of Jerusalem. This Jesus was no danger in Galilee, but here, in Jerusalem, it was a different matter. People were openly saying that he was the prophet Elijah come back to life again. More than that, some even believed that he was the messiah.

He was growing more apprehensive as the time of the Passover drew nigh. The reports of the popularity of Jesus came in tumbling over one another. Then five days before the Feast, he openly declared himself the messiah, and crowds of people were fools enough to believe him. But Caiaphas almost choked with rage when he heard what happened two days later in the Temple. This upstart had thrown down the gauntlet, directly challenged him as the head of the Temple, accused the Lord's anointed high priest of bribery and extortion, "You have made the house of prayer into a den of thieves" [see Matthew 21:13; Mark 11:17; Luke 19:46]. The insolence of it!

From that moment, the viper knew that his whole career was at stake. Suppose the people revolted ... Heaven alone knew what might happen! This Jesus would be the king of the religious castle, and that would be farewell, long farewell to all Caiaphas's greatness! The viper was coiling, ready to strike. His one difficulty was the crowd. He must capture Jesus when he was out of reach of the crowd. He was at his wits' end to know how to catch Jesus, alone, when Judas arrived. And, learning that Jesus spent one time after supper in the lonely garden of Gethsemane, immediately the viper struck.

The important fact is that Caiaphas was in a hurry. In thirty-six hours the Jewish Sabbath would commence. He dare not let Jesus be free for a moment longer. The fuse of popular revolution had already almost burnt to the point of contact. Jesus had to be tried and executed within thirty-six hours if Caiaphas was to save his skin. Understand that, and you will understand the utter travesty of justice which this trial was.

Caiaphas

Frank Morison,[1] the author of *Who Moved the Stone?* spent a lifetime in studying the last seven days of the life of Jesus. And these are his conclusions on the trial. It was from first to last illegal—a put-up job. Let me quote him:

> It was illegal for the Temple Guard ... to effect the arrest. That should have been left to the voluntary action of the witnesses. It was illegal to try a capital charge (trial for life) by night. It was illegal, after the testimony of the witnesses had broken down, for the judges to cross-examine the prisoner. They should have acquitted him, and if the testimony was demonstrably false the witnesses should have been sentenced to death by stoning.

Caiaphas, the upholder of Jewish Law, was to reveal himself as a triple law-breaker in one day. Unscrupulous and venomous viper that he was!

The last words must be about his cunning. He knew that Pilate would not be introduced to his religious charges, so he included a political charge. This Jesus claims to be a king, he said. By that one charge, he implicated Pilate in the plot.

But even then his plans would have failed. Jesus refused to admit anything. He was silent, most embarrassingly silent. Caiaphas had to produce an admission of some kind from him. He played his last card. Rising to his feet in his splendid garments, he demanded that Jesus should say whether he was the Christ, the Son of the living God. "I adjure Thee by the living God that thou confess to us that thou be the Christ" [Matthew 26:63; Mark 14:61; Luke 22:67]. When a loyal Jew was asked the question in the name of God, he could not refuse. And Jesus was a loyal Jew. It is as if a loyal Protestant were asked to swear on the Bible. And notice this: this insincere priest exploited the very sincerity of the prisoner. With this unsavory incident, I close the curtain over a whited sepulcher, a character whose deeds reek of the charnel-house, and smell foul after the winds of twenty centuries have swept across the earth.

Thank God that hypocrisy of such proportions is unknown in the Christian religious life of today. The crucifixion of Jesus has, at any rate, nailed the coffin of hypocrisy in Christian circles.

But you and I would be the veriest blind fools if we could not see the red warning light that flashes from God's Word through Caiaphas. No man sets out to be a hypocrite. He becomes a hypocrite only as his soul deadens:

---

1. Frank Morison, pseudonym of Albert Henry Ross (1881–1950), was an English writer known for *Who Moved the Stone?* (1930).

it is the sleeping-sickness of the soul that attacks the man for whom religion is only a matter of rites, ceremonies, and mere habit, in short, a God-deserting and man-hating religion. There is only one safe precaution against this disease. That is to have the mind of Christ. But that cannot be obtained in a day or a year. It is obtained only by those who believe in Christ with heart and soul, and who act on his teaching, so that their consciences become as sensitive as the flickering tenderness in his eyes, and their love for men as all-embracing as the poor, pierced hands that enfolded the world, including Judas and even Caiaphas.

The King—Herod
The Strain of Christ's Silent Scrutiny

One hymn takes us into the inner meaning of the Cross in two lines:

> O love of God! O sin of man!
> In this dread act your strength is tried.[1]

There is no mistaking the fact that the Cross reveals the diabolical nature of sin. It takes the lid off our human nature, and exposes its brute savagery. Do not tell me that we are kindly human beings, we men. I know that we are beasts. Watch us in the eerie darkness of the Cross, spitting in the face of God, striking, piercing, breaking the heart of the Son of God. The Cross cries, "Shame!" "Shame!" "Shame on the whole race of men!"

We looked into the black heart of one of these beasts this morning, Caiaphas the viper. Tonight we shall, with God's Word, lay bare the very soul of that fox, Herod.

Don't think he hadn't his good points. He was a man in whom the image of God was not completely defaced and utterly distorted. He was cultured. He built in Caesarea a fine new city which was the envy of Jerusalem itself. He had a difficult country to govern in Galilee, and he managed tolerably well. He was even interested in religion, at least to the extent of collecting preachers, as he collected pictures for his palace. He had, which is more than Pilate or Caiaphas had, a conscience.

It is this conscience of his that brings him into the gospel narrative. You remember that he killed John the Baptist. He did. But he couldn't forget it. When he heard that there was a new prophet who performed miracles in Galilee, he wondered, nay, he was afraid that it might be John risen from the grave to haunt him. Others said that Jesus was Elijah, or one of the old

---

1. Frederick William Faber (see n. 2, p. 137 above.). These lines were written in 1849.

prophets, but Herod said, "John has risen, the John I beheaded." Herod was a superstitious man. If ever a man deserved to be haunted and hounded through life for his treachery, it was Herod, not Judas.

Picture the scene. It is the king's birthday, and all night long the country palace of Herod echoes to the high roof with screams of laughter, and the frenzied reeling of music. The shepherd on the crag a mile away hears nothing, but he watches at midnight lights rising from the base of the rocky castle to the top. He sees one window lighting above another and he knows that John the Baptist is being led by his captors from his dank dungeon up the spiral stairs to the banqueting hall. The prophet's time has come, and this mad music is his bitter *requiem*. He advances to the throne where Herod, stupefied with drink and lust, is leering at him with bloodshot eyes. Beside him, nearly naked and certainly unashamed, is Salome, whose whim he is to humor with a prophet's life. Herod speaks, "The queen has taken a fancy to you, John." —"She is no queen; she is not even your wife. She belongs to another man." —"Silence, you rash fool! The queen wants your head to fondle on a silver dish. She shall have it . . . Guards, take him back to his hole and bring me back his head on a silver charger!" [see Matthew 14:6–12; Mark 6:22–29]. And John walked down the steps to death. The musicians stopped their playing, Salome, her dancing, and the whole audience was silent as if its breath had been taken away. For one instant the earth seemed to stand still. The silence was broken by the voice of a ruffian, but it had lost its swagger. He was whimpering. It was not the voice of a king; it was the voice of a lost child.

That story was brought post-haste to Jesus and he replied, "Come away by yourselves to some lonely place and rest!" [Mark 6:31]. The story had taken the zest out of the disciples. Work was impossible for the rest of that day. The greatest of the prophets before Jesus had been annihilated. We cannot know what went on in the mind of Jesus. We can only make a reverent conjecture. Does it strain the imagination too much to believe that Jesus thought of another death, saw another condemned man staggering along the road to death, and heard the same jeering voices. I think not. He knew the diabolical power of evil in the hearts of men.

Some months later, he was himself standing in the presence of Herod. Pilate had sent Jesus to Herod because Jesus was a Galilean, and Herod the Tetrarch of Galilee. Pilate was finding the trial awkward and wanted Herod to take it out of his hands. Herod was flattered by the compliment and glad to be on better terms with the Procurator of Judea. Herod was glad to see

The King—Herod

Jesus. He had conquered his fears that John the Baptist might rise again. He was really delighted to see the latest of the wandering preachers who was drawing such rare audiences. This Jesus was something of a magician too, he was told. Why! There was no telling, he might even perform a miracle to enliven the proceedings. It was with these trivial thoughts in his mind that Herod proceeded to try Jesus. I have not exaggerated the picture. St. Luke gives this very information, "Now when Herod saw Jesus, he was exceeding glad, for he was of a long time desirous to see him, because [of what] he had heard concerning him, and he hoped to see a miracle done by him" [Luke 23:8].

Herod cross-questioned Jesus affably, but pointedly and repeatedly; but Jesus remained absolutely silent. That silence is itself the most illuminating comment on the character of Herod. Such a trivial man could not conduct a trial; what justice could Jesus get from the man who had killed John the Baptist for a pretty dancing girl's request to satisfy her incestuous mother. Jesus remained silent. And weak, affable Herod could not bear the strain of Christ's silent scrutiny; he knew that he was being condemned, not Jesus. He did what evil must do when faced with goodness. He lied to ridicule it, make it appear to be anything but what it was. He made a joke of Jesus to hide his own discomfort. Herod dressed him up in finery and put a crown askew on his head. "Thinks he's a king; a fine king he looks," and sent him back to Pilate in this sorry disguise [see Luke 23:6–11]. And that feeble joke was the last Jesus heard of Herod.

Such was Herod: clever, undoubtedly, and cultured, and interested in religion. But he had one fatal flaw: it was a religion at the top of the mind, not a religion at the root of his will. It was a religion that fought shy of reformation. It was feeble: he wanted God but he wouldn't pay God's price for it. Surely Herod prayed Augustine's pre-conversion prayer a hundred times, "O God, make me chaste, but not yet." He wanted God but he wanted Herodias more; and he had her, although she was his brother's wife, although he was married himself.

Yes, although his legitimate wife's father was a powerful Arab warrior, and might cost him his crown. And in the end, he was deposed by his father-in-law. Herod's fault was not a lack of good intentions; it was a lack of resolution. That moral failure cost John the Baptist his life; and it helped to crucify Jesus, only because he did not lift a finger to vindicate Christ. He knew Jesus was no pretender to his throne. He knew that Jesus was a prophet, whose powers were approved of God by the miracles he wrought. He knew all that, but he sent Jesus back to Pilate and to death.

I do not know any Caiaphas: but I know many Herods today. People without resistance, without moral courage, who had little faith before the war, whose religion was best described as being pallid with the Deity. These fair-weather-friends of the faith have gone: perhaps they will return after the war. Perhaps they will never return.

To you who remain, Christ's words have reality, "Let him that would be my disciple take up his Cross and follow me" [Matthew 16:24; Mark 8:34; Luke 9:23]. You knew religion as consolation; you also know religion as demand, as a challenge to the highest in you, and the best. Surely Jesus will not have to say to you, "Will ye also go away?" [John 6:67]. God forbid. I believe that he will say to you, "Well done, thou good and faithful servant; enter thou into the joy of thy Lord. You have suffered with me; you shall reign with me" [see Matthew 25:21, 23].

And that makes all the agony and the sweat worthwhile, because his hand is on your shoulder now, and your hand will be in his, then. Let the cynical laugh; but let the people of God shout for joy, for now we see in a glass darkly [see 1 Corinthians 13:12], but then, face-to-face. I would give everything in the world to bring a smile to that tortured sad face, to see it light up as the prodigal came home [see Luke 15:11–32], and to hear the bells of heaven chiming as if they would break with sheer joy. Wouldn't you?

Pontius Pilate
He Washes His Hands

Everyone here has heard of *The London Times*, but not many have heard of a much more important newspaper that is called "*The Jerusalem Times.*" *The London Times* seems dear enough at three pence a copy, but *The Jerusalem Times* is priceless. There is only one known copy of it, definitely a first edition, and only part of that has yet appeared. Even in these days, it is highly illustrated in at least three colors, and it employs an editorial staff of at least eight, including an editor, and several special correspondents. It is their duty to interview leading citizens in Galilee and Judea, and they have secured several scoops already. Their articles are written in vivid, racy English. If you want to see a copy, the only existing copy of this famous journal, we are fortunate to possess it in our junior church and you will find it exhibited on the notice board in the passage.

Now for the rest of this service we are going to act as the special legal correspondents of *The Jerusalem Times*. The editor has given us a very important job; today we have to issue a special supplement on a famous trial: the trial of Jesus-ben-Joseph, alias messiah, a carpenter and miracle-worker and teacher, who was condemned to be hung on a cross until he died. One reporter is sent to interview his followers, but they are nowhere to be found. Another is sent to hear the comments of Annas and Caiaphas, the high priests. He comes back with the curt message, "Trouble-maker, danger to the safety of Jerusalem. There'll be no more trouble from him." Another comes back with the astonishing news that a certain Judas, who handed over Jesus to the military police, has killed himself. Our job is to cover Pilate.

We start by investigating his past life. We approach one of his guards. A burly fellow, he is, and very talkative, "I can tell you all about the Procurator

How Far Down Dare I Drink?

. . ." and he does. "Hasn't much time for your squabbles, you know. He put his foot down as soon as he was appointed governor. I remember . . ."

What did he remember? When Pilate and Lady Claudia arrived at Caesarea to take up office, he remembered what a queer determined look there was on his face. A look that went through you, that seemed to say, "I'll teach those Jews a lesson, and that clever Caiaphas who's master here. I stand for Rome, for imperial Rome, and these hotheads in Jerusalem shall see who has the whip-hand." In a few days, he was showing them. He sent his soldiers up to Jerusalem, bearing their flags, and on the flags were the images of the Roman God. The Jews worshipped the one God who had said to Moses, "Thou shalt not make any graven image or likeness of me" [Exodus 20:4]. That would offend their consciences and break their laws. Pilate knew this would cause offence; so he sent the soldiers by night, so that when morning dawned the offensive ensigns would be in the Holy City. There was a popular uproar. Crowds of people besieged Pilate's rooms in Jerusalem and demanded that the ensigns be removed. Pilate endured their ravings for five days and nights.

Then he pretended that he was going to answer their request. He had his seat carried to an open place in front of the palace and he gave secret orders for a detachment of soldiers to hide nearby in readiness. When the crowd began to shout again, he gave orders for the ring-leaders to be surrounded and threatened them with instant death if they would not stop their cries. The leaders bared their necks ready for the executioner's sword, and would have died rather than promise to be silent. Pilate knew that these men had not been put up to annoy him by the high priest: they were sincere and, to his credit, he recognized it. He gave his word that the ensigns should be removed, and he kept it. The crowds left for their homes and there was great rejoicing throughout Judea in the year 26, the first of Pilate's governorship.

Now that is the first report on Pilate. He was masterful and rash, but he had the good sense to know where to draw the line, and to recognize the difference between sincere and insincere men.

That is the first part of the story. Now we interview a rather superior person, dressed in flowing robes. He is a priest. He loathes Pilate, in a dignified way, and is ready to tell us about another incident, this time when Pilate went too far. This is the report we take down from him:

> Pilate made up his mind to improve the water-supply in Jerusalem by linking up the pools of Solomon, up in the hills, by a viaduct

which was forty-seven miles long. And he had the audacity to use our sacred money for it, money used for the upkeep of God's Temple here, given to God by the faithful in Judea and beyond the seas. He was worse than a common robber, for even they leave the sacred treasury alone.

Once the people knew of this theft, and the purpose for which it was to be used, they ran to his house and besieged it, threatening to batter it down. But Pilate, the sly murderer, was ready for them. He gave instruction for the soldiers in the fortress of Antonia to be ready at dawn, to wear civilian dress, and to conceal their arms. If the crowd looks like it is getting out of hand, the soldiers are to quiet them up with a blow of their clubs. The open place is made ready for Pilate's arrival; the disguised soldiers are already mixing in the crowd and Pilate walks down the steps from his official residence to the seat of judgment. Pandemonium reigns: the Jews shout bitter insults at Pilate, wave their arms at him. The Romans, inflamed by the insults, immediately went for the ringleaders. Panic ensued. The huge crowd fled towards the narrow exits, and when these were choked, some stumbled, and they were trodden to death, in the stampede.

And the speaker added:

> If you want my opinion of Pilate, he's a blundering fool and twenty years in Jerusalem won't teach him how to deal with our people. He calls them obstinate. They are religious people and they have the courage of their convictions, which is more than he has.

Now that we have these two reports on Pilate, the soldier's and the priest's, we can see the line he took at the trial. We shall expect him to bluff and to call off his bluff, just as he did in the first story, and as he would like to have done in the second.

In the middle of the night a knock comes on his door. It is Caiaphas, who must see him quickly. The crowds in Jerusalem are seething again. They are threatening to make Jesus of Nazareth a king over them. "It's not only my position I'm thinking of, Procurator; it is yours, too. We must stand together against this impertinent revolutionary." And he adds, "We can't execute him, without your authority. I tell you he's a danger to Rome and to us. I want you to bring in a verdict of guilty; that will be ours. I'll bring him before you early tomorrow."

Next morning the prisoner stood before Pilate. St. John tells us what happened. Pilate questioned the high priest and his company. "What accusation do you bring against this man?" he asks, as if he had heard nothing from Caiaphas the night before. Caiaphas and his men were annoyed; they evaded the question, "If this man were not a lawbreaker, do you think we'd have bothered to bring him before you?"

Pilate then took Jesus into the Palace to question him privately. Pilate asks, "Are you the king of the Jews?" [Matthew 27:11; Mark 15:2; Luke 23:3]. And Jesus tries to make Pilate understand . . . if he is really trying to do justice, "Is this your own conclusion, or have others reported it to you about me?" Pilate makes an ironical answer, "Do you take me for a Jew? Your own countrymen and your own chief priests have handed you over to me. What have you done?" [see John 18:34–35]. Jesus answered, "My kingdom does not belong to this world; if it did, my men would have fought to prevent me being handed over to the Jews. No. My kingdom lies elsewhere." "Then you are a king?" Pilate rejoined. "Most certainly, I am king. That is why I was born. That is why I came into the world, as a witness to the truth. Anyone who belongs to the truth listens to my voice." "Truth" said Pilate, "what does truth mean?" [see John 36–38].

The cross-examination was over. Pilate told the Jews, "I find nothing wrong with him. He is innocent" [see John 18:38]. But now we see the cowardice of this bluff, hearty man. He didn't dare to let Jesus go. He was afraid that Caiaphas would report him to the emperor, Tiberius. Caiaphas threatened him, "If you let this man go, you are not Caesar's friend" [John 19:12]. That might mean banishment. Anything but that!

Now watch the way Pilate shelves his responsibility. First he says, "All right then, try him yourselves" [see John 19:6]. He knew they would; but they had no authority to put Jesus to death. Only the Governor could ratify the death sentence.

Then he tries another approach, "He's a Jew. Send this king of the Jews to the other king. Send him to Herod."

He makes a last attempt to shift the responsibility onto other shoulders, "You know that I have a right to free a prisoner today. Do you want Barabbas or Jesus?" The crowd chooses Barabbas [see Matthew 27:17; Mark 1511; Luke 23:18; John 18:40]. He makes a last feeble attempt at evasions. He tells the soldiers to whip Jesus, and when he cannot be heard above the shouting, he calls for a basin of water, and washes his hands, to show that he is innocent of the fate of Jesus [see Matthew 27:24].

Pilate has declared Jesus innocent, but he will not let him go because he fears he will lose his position. He washes his hands of the whole affair.

Pontius Pilate

But he has a last joke. He writes on the placard which will be put on the cross as a warning to evil-doers, "The king of the Jews" [see John 19:19–21]. The priests urge him to alter it to read, "He said that he was the king of the Jews." But obstinate Pilate would not budge, "What I have written, I have written" [John 19:22]. He dismisses the whole trial with a witticism. He makes a joke of the death of an innocent man.

And so Jesus went to the cross, because of the weakness of Pilate, who did not dare to be true to his convictions. The verdict of Pilate on Jesus was, "Not Guilty." But the verdict of Caiaphas was, "Guilty, sentenced to death," and Pilate handed him over, against his conscience.

No doubt, if there had been a *Jerusalem Times*, in those days, it would have agreed with the high priest. And it would have headed its legal article: "Deserved Death of a Revolutionary, Sorcerer, and Blasphemer." And that would have been the last we should have heard of Jesus. A few friends of his would have repeated the story of his trial and death to their children. But within sixty years, the story would have been forgotten.

Then how is it that we are meeting in a church today and singing the praises of a crucified Jewish criminal, whom the Jews and Romans of his time thought they had killed? How is it that we even know that he was crucified at all? The Jews wouldn't want the story spread. What was one criminal crucified amongst so many? The disciples wouldn't. They were keeping quiet, locked in a room away from the crowds, where they hoped that Caiaphas and his men wouldn't ferret them out. If the disciples and the Jews didn't want to spread the story of the crucified prophet, who did?

The answer is: Jesus himself. Jesus, guilty in the eyes of men, was declared innocent by God. God brought him back from the dead again and told the world, "This is my beloved son in whom I am well pleased. Hear ye him!" [Matthew 3:17; Mark 1:11; Luke 3:22].

The City Counselor, Joseph of Arimathea
A Deserter in Bed
Kindness Without Courage

> When it was evening, there came a rich man from Arimathea, named Joseph, who also was a disciple of Jesus. He went to Pilate and asked for the body of Jesus. Then Pilate ordered it to be given to him. And Joseph took the body, and laid it in his own new tomb, which he had hewn in the rock; and he rolled a great stone to the door of the tomb, and departed. (Matthew 27:57–60)

> And when evening had come, since it was the day of Preparation, that is, the day before the Sabbath, Joseph of Arimathea, a respected member of the council, who was also himself looking for the kingdom of God, took courage and went to Pilate, and asked for the body of Jesus. And Pilate wondered if he were already dead; and summoning the centurion, he asked him whether he was already dead. And when he learned from the centurion that he was dead, he granted the body to Joseph. And he bought a linen shroud, and taking him down, wrapped him in the linen shroud, and laid him in a tomb which had been hewn out of the rock, and he rolled a stone against the door of the tomb. (Mark 15:42–46)

> Now there was a man named Joseph from the Jewish town of Arimathea. He was a member of the council, a good and righteous man, who had not consented to their purpose and deed, and he was looking

The City Counselor, Joseph of Arimathea

for the kingdom of God. This man went to Pilate and asked for the body of Jesus. Then he took it down and wrapped it in a linen shroud, and laid him in a rock-hewn tomb, where no one had ever yet been laid. (Luke 23:50–53)

After this Joseph of Arimathea, who was a disciple of Jesus, but secretly, for fear of the Jews, asked Pilate that he might take away the body of Jesus, and Pilate gave him leave. So he came and took away his body. Nicodemus also, who had at first come to him by night, came bringing a mixture of myrrh and aloes, about a hundred pounds' weight. They took the body of Jesus, and bound it in linen cloths with the spices, as is the burial custom of the Jews. Now in the place where he was crucified there was a garden, and in the garden a new tomb where no one had ever been laid. So because of the Jewish day of Preparation, as the tomb was close at hand, they laid Jesus there. (John 19:38–42)

If we are to see the real Joseph of Arimathea, the city counselor of Jerusalem, holding office in the year A.D. 33, then we must take off the rose-colored spectacles of fancy. Mediaeval devotion and English patriotism have converted a decent man into an improbable saint. It would be delightful to believe that Joseph came over to England in the year 63, bringing with him the golden chalice of the Last Supper; that he set up a simple church of mud and wattles in still unspoiled Somerset, in ancient Glastonbury. But if you are searching for truth, beware of guide-books, especially of publicity agents with a flair for the romantic. The more sober truth about Joseph is found in the Book of Books. Joseph was not the kind of man to undertake a pilgrimage to a barbaric and desolate spot, which would take years to complete, and he was probably already in his seventies, if not in his eighties, at that time. Moreover, Jesus, in all probability, did not drink from a golden chalice, but from a wooden cup made from the trunk of a sycamore. And, as you will see later, Joseph was no dauntless explorer or missionary; he was a timid man.

We must look at him as he appears in the gospels. We do not hear much about him; his life is written in three or four verses in each of the four gospels. But we can build up a vivid picture from these four converging searchlights. St. Mark's searchlight reveals him as a counselor of good position," "one of those who waited for the reign of God." "He ventured to go to Pilate and ask for the body of Jesus" which "he laid in the tomb" in his own garden. That searchlight alone reveals that he is a respectable man, a man of prayer, a kindly man, and, in his way, brave for such a sensitive person. St. Matthew adds that he was a rich man. St. Luke says that he was "a member of the council," (the Sanhedrin) "but a good and just man who had not voted for their plan of action." But the most vivid searchlight of all comes from St. John. He says, and this reveals the hidden fear in the man, as hideously as a searchlight discovers an enemy plane, he says, "Joseph of Arimathea, a disciple of Jesus, but a secret disciple, for fear of the Jews."

We fit these pieces in a jig-saw puzzle together and the whole shows us a rich, respectable, kindly, but timid man who recovered his courage sufficiently to become momentarily an avowed disciple of Jesus.

I want you to picture the events of Holy Week from the stand-point of this city counselor. He was a native of Arimathea, the town high up in the hills some thirty miles from Jerusalem to the North-West. But, small and secluded as this town was, it was famous as the birthplace of a great prophet, Samuel. And Joseph was the leading citizen, with a seat on the exclusive Sanhedrin which, under Caiaphas, ruled the Jews of Judaea and the Dispersion. Joseph probably thought that Jesus was a second Samuel, and greater than Samuel. He was one of the little band of quietists who like Simeon and Anna were daily expecting the advent of the messiah. He "waited for the kingdom of God." He had heard of Jesus and was even impressed by the reports of his teaching and the astonishing miracles he had performed. He was in Jerusalem during the days preceding the Passover, probably staying with another counselor and his wife. He had seen the tributes of the populace on the Sunday, when Jesus rode through their midst, and it seemed the certain answer to his prayers. Now Jerusalem would have a real prophet to lead her instead of cunning old Caiaphas: a leader approved by the people and by God, not a time-server. On the Tuesday, when Jesus turned over the money-changers in the Temple, Joseph must have thought: "This is the new order. Caiaphas is doomed. It is only a matter of hours now. Friday will see Jesus of Nazareth holding the reins of power. Meanwhile, Joseph, if you're a sensible man, you'll lie low. Jesus knows that you're on his side. No public demonstrations are necessary. Stay at home, except for your regular visits to the Temple for prayers. Caiaphas is already overthrown. There's no point in incurring his enmity. Lie low, Joseph. . ." He had retired early as usual on Thursday night, and was fast asleep. In the early hours of Friday morning,

The City Counselor, Joseph of Arimathea

there was a savage, insistent rap at the door. Joseph turned over. Was it another nightmare? No, it was real hammering, and no mistake. He flung a cloak over his shoulders and descended.

At the door was a breathless emissary of Caiaphas. "Sorry to trouble you, sir, at this time of night but the high priest sends his compliments and summons you to attend an extraordinary meeting of the Council. He says it is a life-or-death-matter, sir."

"Life-or-death-matter?" (He thought death for Caiaphas, but not for Jesus). "Tell him" he said, "I've never heard of such a thing as a trial by night. Tell him it is illegal. I'll be no party to it. God be with you." "Good night, sir." It was a bad night for Joseph of Arimathea; back again in bed a sinister voice was saying "Lie low, Joseph... There's nothing to worry about... Lie low!" But that voice wouldn't send him to sleep. Another voice, quieter was saying, "Blessed are ye when men shall persecute you and revile you and say all manner of evil against you falsely for my sake, for great is your reward in heaven. [Matthew 5:11–12; Luke 6:22–23]. Joseph, are you my disciple?" And Joseph answered, "It's all very well for fishermen to follow you openly, but I have my position to think of. I'm with you all right. I'll be out in the open tomorrow to see your success."

But tomorrow dawned, and a hideously black Friday. It was a failure. Jesus put up no resistance. He simply let Caiaphas, and Herod, and Pilate have their way. This revolutionary prophet was like the rest, except that he put up less fight than the others. He simply died. And Joseph's hopes died with him. But Joseph was a sensitive man; he couldn't bear to think that Jesus should be thrown into the common pit with a couple of common thieves. He deserved a better end than that. He would bury Jesus in the orchard in which his own tomb was ready. These last offices of decency should be observed. He would pay the tribute of a friend, even if it meant approaching Pilate and offending the Sanhedrin.

We do not deny courage; we must only regret that it came too late. He used both hands to bury Jesus, but he didn't lift a finger to keep him alive. Then the curtain drops on a private funeral, and that is the last we hear of Joseph of Arimathea.

In the moving, human story of this city counselor, there lies the Word of God for us. God teaches us, that decency is not enough. Kindness may be lovely, but ineffectual.

Joseph was kindness itself. He wouldn't harm anyone. He was sensitive. He recoiled at the ugly thought of the corpse of Jesus being flung to rot in a muddy pit on the hillside. He had a beautiful garden in the Holy City, quiet and secluded. In it lay the brand new tomb which he had ordered for himself. The earthly remains of Jesus should repose there. Despite Caiaphas and the Sanhedrin, who would certainly expel him, he would perform the last offices of tenderness. He would embalm the Savior and weep sadly as he committed him to what he thought would be the last resting-place. He was kind; make no mistake.

But kindness, if it is not allied with moral courage is weak, pitiably weak. His kindness came too late. It would have been kinder to Christ to have protested against the illegality of his trial in the Sanhedrin, kinder to risk displeasure, kinder to fight the good fight, and not to be a deserter in bed. It was a hard choice to make: he had a lot to lose, but he was to lose more in refusing the costly choice. Explain it; but you cannot explain away the fact that he consented to the death of Jesus. He might say, "I had nothing to do with it." But he could not say, "I did everything to stop it."

His tragedy was kindness without courage. It is ours, too. He was a believer, yet secretly, for fear of the Jews. O Christians, don't those words strike home? Believer . . . Secretly . . . For fear. Joseph was on the fringe of discipleship. Are you? It is the secrecy that lets Christ down. I don't suggest that you hide the fact that you come to church. The world regards that as perfectly harmless, a mere eccentric hobby on our part, like collecting old coins, or rare prints, or first editions. The world doesn't mind your kindness. There are thousands of kind people about, neighbors who will share their shelter with you, odd travelers on the train who will hand round their cigarettes, even in these days. The world is only offended when you suggest that it needs to be changed, when you assert that this Jesus of Nazareth was God incarnate, and that he holds the destiny of the universe in his hands . . . when you interfere with people. It is then that the opposition starts. Young people, in your first jobs, you find that you are thought to be a goody-goody because you are a Christian. I can imagine how you feel. I have heard the sneers, "Little innocent; he doesn't know the ways of the world. We'll teach him to be a sport." I know the angry uprush of feeling that has to be stayed and the sense of isolation. I know, too, the magnificent sense of achievement, of knowing that this is our testing time, that if I am ever called a good sport or a broad-minded fellow, they want to win me over to their side, to drag me down to their level, to dirty my soul with their smuttiness. This is my supreme chance of witnessing. Older people, immersed in business, working with others who are men and women of the

The City Counselor, Joseph of Arimathea

world, holding positions of responsibility, I know that you too have to face ridicule. Perhaps, the others do not laugh openly, they may just whisper, or they may soften their taunts by suggesting that you are old-fashioned, or narrow, or an old fogey, or sub-normal to believe all that stuff, or that you have a kink.

Young, old, or middle-aged, these taunts are the very devil's vocabulary; you know it, and happy are you if you recognize it; happier still are you if you can say, "I am a believer," openly and fearlessly. If you can say, what Joseph would have given anything to say, "I'm not ashamed to own my Lord Or to defend his cause."

Happy? Nay, blessed are ye since louder than the jeers, you hear a strong encouraging voice. Blessed are ye when men shall hate you and when they shall separate you from their company, and reproach you, and cast out your name for evil, for the son of man's sake. Rejoice in that day and leap for joy [see Matthew 5:11–12; Luke 6:22–23].

If you can do that, then you are an open believer, a veritable apostle of Jesus Christ.

O Jesus Christ, my Lord and friend, enter into my soul, and drive out all fears of what others think of me, and make my only desire to gain and keep thy divine approval. AMEN.

The Soldier—Longinus
You Are the Centurion

Only one man saw Jesus die, and his remark was almost commonplace, "Certainly, this was a righteous man" [Luke 23:47]. Then, why does this man deserve a sermon all to himself? First because of the kind of man he was; secondly because of the situation which produced the remark.

What kind of man was he, then? He was a Roman centurion. We should call him a company sergeant or a captain. He was a non-commissioned officer of some importance and he was in charge of a hundred men. Yes, but even that doesn't tell us a great deal about him. We must look for other evidence in the gospels for what kind of men these non-commissioned Roman officers were. Then we discover an unexpected fact. The apostles and their Lord had a very high opinion of centurions. Jesus met one of them in Capernaum. He was a most considerate man, a man without prejudices, and a man who recognized authority when he saw it. Considerate? Oh yes, he'd come to fetch Jesus to heal his paralyzed servant. Without prejudices? He was a Roman officer approaching a Jewish teacher. "Sir," he said, "I am not fit to have you under my roof" [Matthew 8:8; Luke 5:6]. A man who recognized the authority of Jesus? "Only say the word and my servant will be healed" [Matthew 8:8; Luke 5:7]. This man evoked a tremendous compliment from Jesus, "I tell you truly I have not met faith like this anywhere in Israel" [Matthew 8:10; Luke 5:9]. That was our Lord's opinion of one sergeant-major.

Turn to the Acts of the Apostles (10:1–31), and you will find that the apostles held the same opinion of centurions. We are told of Cornelius that he was "a good man who reverences God and is highly esteemed by the whole Jewish nation." A Roman, a member of the race of overlords, held in high esteem by the Jews, he became a Christian convert.

The Soldier—Longinus

Seventeen chapters later (Acts 27), we come across Julius, another centurion. We are told that, at Sidon, "Julius very courteously allowed Paul to visit his friends and be looked after" [Acts 27:3].

Three centurions, Cornelius, Julius and the soldier at the Cross, whom tradition names Longinus, every one of them is mentioned with approval. Is it simply that they were three exceptions? The truth is surely that these men were representatives of a fine type of officer in those days. They were all disciplinarians; they had to be or their men would be insubordinate, and the Jews would revolt. They were all men of courage; they were armed, it is true, but they were greatly outnumbered by a race that would risk its life if it thought its religious liberties were imperiled. They were courteous, the military ambassadors of a very tolerant empire. Longinus was that kind of man, a disciplinarian, a courageous man, a man of honor, and a courteous man, but a man who had to obey orders.

THE SITUATION.

On Good Friday I do not suppose he was over-worried by his commission. He was used to these things. He didn't faint at the sight of blood, and Jesus was to him simply another revolutionary prisoner that he had to put to sleep, though crucifixion was more of a nightmare than a sleep. He watched our blessed Lord stagger under the weight of the Cross and gave orders that Simon of Cyrene should carry it for him. The prisoner was not shamming, obviously. He saw them lay the cross flat on the ground of the ever-sacred hillock of Calvary. He watched the unresisting master lie on the cross while the soldiers drove the nails through his wrists into the wood. He saw them hoist the cross into the socket, and fill up the rest of the hole with dirt. He heard the spitting and jeering of the crowd; he watched his own men toss up for the prisoner's seamless robe. He heard the robber cry and curse from the other cross. He heard only seven sayings from the Central Cross.

But listen to them. They are the words of the crucified Son of God, words preached, not from the comfort of a pulpit, but from the agony, and loneliness, and disappointment of the Cross, words that came from a racked and tortured frame, words from a still center of faith in the midst of the whirlwind of hatred, and lies, and disloyalty. Hear these words, for they are the words of God incarnate, speaking to the world that had conspired to murder him.

How Far Down Dare I Drink?

"Father, forgive them for they know not what they do" [Luke 23:34]. Hear the pity in them for you Caiaphas, for Judas, for Joseph of Arimathea, for the disciples, for you, for every soul that is burdened with a sensitive conscience, for those who arrested him, for Longinus ... "Father, forgive them for they know not what they do."

Now he turns to speak to the penitent thief, "Verily I say unto thee, today thou shalt be with me in paradise" [Luke 23:43]. The friend of sinners continues his blessed work of love to the last. It was the robber's last moment and it was his last moment. The robber died in peace, with the promise of Christ on his lips. You can die tomorrow in peace, if you die in penitence. "Verily I say unto thee, today thou shalt be with me in paradise."

He is still thinking of others. There is little strength left in his wounded body, but he uses it for Mary and John: "Woman, behold thy son ... Behold thy Mother" [John 19:26]. Mary will be looked after by John, and John will have the best of mothers to care for him.

The agony is almost unbearable, "I thirst" [John 19:28], the Savior cries. But he will not accept the drugs they offer him. He must bear the agony of it, until death releases him. This is no suicide. He is bearing the sins of the world [see John 1:29; 1 Peter 2:24]. The bitterness of sin must not be dulled. Now the delirium has set in. But even now, faith is holding the anchor. "My God, my God, why hast thou forsaken me?" [Matthew 27:46; Mark 15:34]. The bystanders hear him quoting Psalm 22 [22:1], but the rest of it is inaudible. They do not hear its triumphant conclusion. "He hath not despised nor abhorred the affliction of the afflicted. Neither hath he hid his face from him but when he cried unto him" [Psalm 22:24] he heard. Amid the shadows that wheeled like vultures through his soul, he saw clearly the face of God, the Father.

Death was very near now. But he summoned his final energies. Then, as if for the benefit of the centurion who was brushing his lips with a sponge soaked in vinegar, he said, "It is finished" [John 19:30]. He needed no more human kindness, but he was grateful.

Then, as the soul was leaving its battered prison, he spoke with the trumpet-voice of faith. He had been through the deep waters but now he could see the land, the land of his Father, and on that limitless shore stood God. "Father into thy hands I commit my spirit" [Luke 23:46].

The centurion alone had seen and heard the last act of the drama of our salvation. And he, a Roman official and executioner, gave his verdict,

The Soldier—Longinus

"Certainly this was a righteous man" [Luke 23:47] or, as the other gospels put it, "Certainly this was a Son of God" [Matthew 27:54; Mark 15:39].

He had come to arrest Jesus, and the Lord had arrested him. And this unprejudiced man, this soldier about the Cross, paid his testimony, "Certainly this was a righteous man." It was the sober verdict of the man in uniform.

This honest centurion is a first-rate witness to the power of the Cross. And he can teach us two very important lessons.

The first one is to be absolutely honest about our religion. He did not go beyond his own experience of truth in Christ. He would not say that Jesus was a criminal, even though the Lord was condemned as such. Neither would he say that Jesus was the messiah. He said simply what he had seen, "This man was certainly a righteous man, a Son of God." No one made him say it. He saw the truth for himself. Others were to see deeper into the truth later. Others at the time were to distort the truth by their prejudices. But Longinus had begun aright the journey that leads to Christ. He reported his impressions honestly.

All of you, in this congregation, are probably at different stages of discipleship. Some have been in the faith for over half a century. Some are taking the first halting steps. But believers, old or new, you have to take the same path over the rickety bridge of faith to certainty. Sometimes the bridge will sway; you will lean over towards modern science, or on the other side, towards ancient doubt; but if you go one step at a time and keep your face steadily fixed on the crucified Christ, you will get there; you will find certainty, the certainty of his forgiveness, and the certainty of his promises. Some find certainty early, some find it late; but all honest seekers find him or are found by him.

Don't worry for the moment if some of the biblical records suggest doubts. Don't be troubled if all the hymns do not express your religious emotions. If you can say, "Certainly this was a righteous man," the finest man who ever lived, then your foot is on the right bridge, the bridge of faith. One step is enough for you to begin with, as long as it is an honest step.

The second thing that the centurion teaches is that the testimonial of the common man counts. The truest verdict on the cross was not spoken by Pilate, by Herod, even by the disciples at this time. It was the verdict of the man in the street. Both sides might be expected to have an axe to grind. But the centurion's judgment was impartial. That is why it carries weight.

How Far Down Dare I Drink?

There was another impartial man like the centurion in the gospel. His testimony carried weight, because it was unbiased and honest. He was born blind, and Jesus cured him. The authorities told him that Jesus was not an authorized healer, but a sinner. The man bluntly replied, "I don't know whether he's a sinner or not. One thing I know, once I was blind, and now I see" [John 9:25].

My friends, you are not all expected to be able to argue theologically or philosophically. But you are expected to give your testimonial to the Lord of life. You are that blind man, and you can say, "One thing I know. I was blind to the meaning of life; but now I can see it. He gave me new sight."

You are the centurion. You may not be able to outwit the very clever people in argument, but you have the conviction that no one can take away from you, "This is the Son of God." This life that Christ lived and died for, the life of sacrifice is the most deeply satisfying life. It is the life God wants us to live.

It is on your experience of the grace of God, and on your communicating it that the future of the church depends. "As my Father hath sent me, so send I you" [John 20:21]. That is the command which even the centurion had to obey, which every good soldier of Jesus Christ knows as his marching orders. And he responds:

> Lord speak to me that I may speak
> In living echoes of thy tone;
> As Thou hast sought, so let me seek
> Thy erring children lost and lone.[1]

---

1. Frances Ridley Havergal (1836–1879) was an English poet and hymn writer ("Lord, Speak to Me," 1872).

PART THREE

Faith and Art
Alive to the Color and Glory of the Universe

Faith and Fine Art
Loving God, Loving Art

Preached at Parker Memorial Church, Lehigh University, Bethlehem, Pennsylvania, the fifth Sunday in Lent, March 27, 1966

Exodus 20: 1–20, Colossians 1: 9–19[1]

You shall not make for yourself a graven image, or any likeness of anything that is in heaven above, or that is in the earth beneath, or that is in the water under the earth... (Exodus 20:4)

[The Son] is the image of the invisible God, the first-born of all creation; for in him all things were created, in heaven and on earth, visible and invisible... all things were created through him and for him. He is before all things, and in him all things hold together. (Colossians 1:15–17)

This is a large topic—the relation of Religion and Visual Art—but my aim in discussing it is a very modest one: the hope of allaying suspicion between those who love God, and those who love art. I think it is worth analyzing the nature of the suspicion in the hope of dispelling it.

First, let's look for evidence that theologians and artists are not on speaking terms. The proof will be found in almost any Jewish Synagogue,

---

1. The extended texts indicated here are not quoted. The indicated Exodus text includes the so-called "Ten Commandments." I say "so-called" because these "commandments" are perhaps more appropriately understood as guidelines for freedom. I have selected one verse. From Colossians I have chosen three verses.

Protestant Meeting-house, and, to a lesser degree, in a Catholic Church. What do these dull buildings, these trite conventional erections, say to our imaginations? These are some of the things they say to me. The Protestant Meeting-house in the Puritan tradition says, "The God we worship finds color dangerous. He prefers the black and white of carefully etched lives to the color and sprawl of individuality." The Methodist Church, with its curdled milk stained-glass windows, says, "My haloed Jesus was a safe, warm, sentimental Savior; irrelevant for the daily world of crises, but fine for the family on Sundays." The Presbyterian Church, with its deliberate absence of the historic symbols of Christianity, says through its cubes, diamonds, squares, triangles, circles, and fleurs-de-lys, "I believe in geometry." The plain Jewish Synagogue, as free of symbolism—with the exception of the Star of David—as the Presbyterian, or the Baptist Church, says, "Our God is to be served in the Community; beauty is a distraction." The Roman Catholic Church says, "We will use art for the purposes of religious propaganda, to remind you, by our images of Christ, the Virgin, and the saints, of your duty through these examples." And as we listen, we think, "How very conventional these statues are; we've seen them repeated in plastic in a supermarket a thousand times."

In all these generalizations that I have made, it should be clear that there is a profound suspicion of art in religion. Bishops are as suspicious of creative artists as they are of bikinis, and for the same reason: they suspect them of immorality. So, the negative reaction is taken of eliminating art, or conventionalizing and trivializing art.

But we have only to look outside the synagogues and churches to find artists of genius and originality celebrating the glories or agonies of the creation, enabling us to see as if for the first time.[2]

Let me take the treatment of Jacob Epstein[3] as one very interesting example of the suspicion of religious groups towards a very gifted artist. Here was a New York Jew brought up in great poverty and strict orthodoxy, with a gift for art. His religion, according to Exodus 20:4, reported God as saying from out of the thundering trembling of Mount Sinai, "You shall have no other god before me. You shall not make for yourselves any graven images." And here is the paradox: this man whose religion told him not to make graven images of God, or of God's creation, has lived for nothing else

---

2. See Horton Davies and Hugh Davies, *Sacred Art in a Secular Century* (Collegeville, Minnesota: The Liturgical Press, 1978).

3. Sir Jacob Epstein (1880–1959).

Faith and Fine Art

than making superb, monumental, graven images. No Christian artist in our time has succeeded better than he in making the Bible come alive in towering ways.[4] As Rouault,[5] in painting, has produced a haunting image of Christ, so has Sir Jacob produced at least three major images of Christ that will impose their authority on the imaginations of centuries to come. I am referring to his great *Madonna and Child* in Cavendish Square, London; his tremendous *Ecce Homo* which will one day stand outside St. Paul's Cathedral, London; and his subtle and immense *Christ in Glory* which dominates the upper air in the Cathedral Church of Cardiff, the capital of Wales.

Yes, it is out of the religious organizations that the greatest religious works of art are being done in our time. There is that superb painter and stained-glass expert, another Jew, Chagall. What a rainbow of a palette he uses, and how his lovers and brides seem to levitate without wings in their brimming joy! He has not only constructed stained-glass windows for the new great hospital in Israel, but, more remarkably, for the cathedrals of Rheims and Metz in France. It is becoming respectable to employ those who once were disrespectable.

If my evidence is at all fair, it shows both sides of the suspicion: of the synagogues and churches that are afraid or unwilling to employ the services of distinguished artists, and the fact that distinguished artists cannot stop themselves from producing religious art, whether they have a formal connection with religion or not.

What were the historical roots of this suspicion that the fine arts have no role to play in religion? I think we can fairly say that the roots of this suspicion were and are three dangers which art can create for genuine religion.

The first is, of course, idolatry. The book of Genesis reports that the highest dignity of man is that he was made in the image of God [see Genesis 1:26]. A cynical historian looking at the more sleazy pages of the book of the centuries would add: and man returned the compliment, creating God in the image of man. Gods and goddesses in neighboring Canaan were reduced to fertility principles, and religious art outside Judea was often not much more than the use of phallic symbols as an invitation to immorality or fertility. Even the gods and goddesses of the Homeric epics are no more than human virtues and vices writ large upon Mount Olympus, and the more thoughtful Greek tragedians wanted to banish them from

---

4. See the difficulties the artist encounters in Chaim Potok, *My Name Is Asher Lev* (New York: Alfred A. Knopf, 1972).

5. See n. 4, p. 18 above.

consciousness, for noble men and women were better than these deities of myth and magic.

So fine a sense of the transcendence, and majesty, and mystery of God had the Jewish people that they realized that all images of God were caricatures. So the Holy of Holies in the Temple at Jerusalem was imageless darkness and when men had a sense of God, the [creator], they could only speak of dazzling light, and overwhelming and stunning glory.

In the same tradition, the early Christians followed the Jews (and indeed it should never be forgotten that the earliest Christians were Jews) and because they had no images, they were accused by the Romans of being atheists. And, may I remind you that both the Moslems and the Byzantine or Orthodox Christians of the east, held by the ten commandments, developed a two-dimensional art to keep the commandments, the one arabesque and calligraphic but multi-colored, and the other iconic, two-dimensional pictures, but never sculptures. The Eastern Orthodox, however, believed that the prohibition not to make graven images did not prevent them from making sacred two-dimensional, and ungraven, or uncarved images. They pointed to the undoubted fact that in the New Testament, 1:15 said of Jesus the messiah that "he is," I quote exactly, "the image (*eikōn*) of the invisible God." So, the theologians of the Greek Church followed this clue so carefully that St. Athanasius,[6] as important in the East as St. Augustine in the West, in his great work, *The Incarnation of the Word of God*, said that, because men had so long gone astray in worshipping false gods in idols, God had taken pity on men, and sent them at ground level where their eyes were glued to the true image to end all idols. You can hear, in the final chapters of this treatise, the smashing of idols all over the Roman empire and the departing of the demons, in tribute to the true portrait of the living God, Jesus Christ—God's wisdom in the flesh. So the authority for Christian art was the belief that God constructed his own image, Christ, to restore the sullied human image. Thus it is in the Eastern Church in Greece, Cyprus, Russia, and Romania that we have a marvelous tradition of icon-painting. In Orthodox worship, these icons are the message of salvation to the eye, as the words of the liturgy are to the ear. But note! Icons are highly stylized art: there is no realism in them; they are the anonymous products of monastic groups and so, romantic individuality is ruled out; and they present not the transient and the temporary, but the timeless truth: Mary forever giving the incarnate Christ to the world; Christ with hand forever raised in blessing,

---

6. St. Athanasius of Alexandria (c. 296–373).

Faith and Fine Art

and his Testament in his hand; with all the saints having their piercing eyes that haunt and the golden background that declares they are forever holding high festival in heaven.

Yet the fear of idolatry has lived on in history. In the seventh century, the Eastern Orthodox Church was torn apart by the Iconoclasts, the icon-breakers. In the twelfth century that great monk, St. Bernard of Clairvaux,[7] protested against the unsuitability of worshipping a Christ who lived simply and unpossessively, in gorgeous churches with bejeweled crucifixes. And the sixteenth century Puritans in England and America banished all symbolism from their churches as idolatry and "will-worship."

The second root that causes theologians to be suspicious of art is the great danger of freezing the understanding of God by artistic representation. God who is the ground of being, the ever-energizing creator, is necessarily invisible and any representation of him is a misrepresentation. But even if we admit this, then, even accepting Christ as the image of the invisible God, we would have to acknowledge the dangers of fixing, freezing, and finalizing one aspect of Christ to the neglect of the rest.

It is a fact that different centuries have presented different stereotypes of Christ. The earliest picture was Christ, the good shepherd. There is also Christ, the logos —the eternal wisdom and mighty judge, enthroned in the arch of the Byzantine and domes of churches. There is yet another Christ, the man of sorrows [see Isaiah 53:3], wearing the crown of thorns, fully identified with humanity in its sufferings. There are the more recent representations of Christ: Christ, the workman and friend of working man, a kind of socialist carpenter. There is Christ, latest of all, the atheist who is fully identified with man in the cry of dereliction on the cross, "My God, my God, why have you forsaken me?" [Matthew 27:46; Mark 15:34].

Which is the true Christ? Art's danger is to fix one moment or interpretation as final, and to make the finite absolute.

The third root of the suspicion that fogs the relationships of religion and art is the sense that art is a dangerous distraction in the spiritual life. There is the feeling that art stresses the lust of the eye and the pride of the flesh, whereas the life of the spirit is not aesthetic, but ascetic. What a long history this suspicion has! You can see it in Augustine's[8] *Confessions* when the saint reflects on the cauldron of illicit loves that, [when he attended] plays in Carthage, stirred up and inflamed his imagination. There

---

7. St. Bernard of Clairvaux (1090–1153).
8. Aurelius Augustine of Hippo (354–430).

was the bonfire that the dominican friar, Savonarola,[9] required the people of Florence to burn their vanities in, and which included some of their masterpieces. It is the same suspicion which enables John Wesley[10] to look at the great mediaeval west front of Norwich cathedral, with all its statues of the saints, and to comment on how much money could have been spared and given to the poor. It is also a long-faced feeling that genuine religion is only to be serious and miserable, and never joyful; like the remark of Leslie Stephen's[11] father that he had only smoked one cigar in his life, but that he enjoyed it so passionately he knew he must never, never indulge again. The implications of all this is that true religion lies in the love of man for God's sake, never in the love of beauty. That religion is what you give up, not what you gain.

What are we to say of all these causes for suspicion? I would say this: we must recognize the reality of all these dangers and potential abuses; but the positive response is not to abolish because we may abuse. Luther[12] was asked the same question and he said, "Astrology and prostitution are abuses; but could we abolish the stars, and who would dare to try to abolish women!"

On the much more positive side I would say:

1. In making man in God's own image, God was prepared to take the risk of idolatry; and in the incarnation, he has allowed us to see the icon to end all icons, the Word of God made flesh, full of grace and truth. And the heart of the Christian life is to follow that living image of God's intentions until we are more and more conformed to his likeness.

2. What we need is not less images, but more of them, the more the merrier, because we are then less likely to accept one final interpretation of the relevance of Christ. We can begin by appreciating the splendor of the divine infant in the medieval triptychs of Botticelli[13] or Hans Memling, in which we see a celestial Queen Mary, with stars in her crown, bearing in her lap the universal prince of the people. We can wonder at the incredible beauty of Jesus in Raphael's[14] depiction of him, or the perfect Greek

---

9. Girolamo Savonarola (1452–1498).

10. John Wesley (1703–1791).

11. Leslie Stephens (1832–1904) was an English author and mountaineer—and the father of Virginia Woolf.

12. Martin Luther (1483–1546).

13. Sandro Botticelli (1445–1510).

14. Raphael (1483–1520).

proportions of Christ's human beauty in Michelangelo's *Pieta*.[15] Then we can penetrate the significance of the incarnation in the chiaroscuro of Rembrandt,[16] when he shows us that the real glory of Christ's descent to earth was its humility—a manger or a byre for a birthplace, and simple peasants for companions—and that the meaning of it all is not a temporary slumming on earth, but enabling men to penetrate the incognito of who Christ was: the recognition that this crucified "criminal" is God's greatest gift to the alienated. This is the depiction of faith: the glory in the commonplace, so that what began in Palestine may enter into every human heart.

3. The true life of religion is for the whole personality, for body as well as soul, for feelings as well as will, for the imagination as well as the intellect. This means that we must be open to all the creativity of the supreme artist who paints sunsets and roses, who stripes the tigers and zebras, and forms the poignant loveliness of human beauty, too.

Above all it means that neither Puritanism, nor Pietism, nor the parochialism of denominationalism, must prevent us from seeing that God is for the world, not for one religion, and certainly not only for the saved.[17] With God, the unexpected is always happening, so that in the mid-twentieth century, the best Christian interpreters are a peasant pope, voted into the supreme position as a stop-gap, who revolutionizes the Catholic Church, and a Jewish sculptor, Epstein, whose imagination is haunted by the gigantic biblical forms, and who haunts us with a God-sized Christ in place of the cardboard Christ's of our own timid devising. The artists will show us that our God is too small!

---

15. Michelangelo Buonarroti (1475–1564). The *Pieta* is from 1498–1499.

16. Rembrandt Harmenszoon van Rijn (1606–1669).

17. This remarkable declaration reveals the heart of Horton Davies. With all of the staunch particularity of his affirmation of Christianity (and precisely through it!), he reaches out to embrace the universal. See below, "The Value of Modern Fiction for Preachers," pp. 172–181.

The Value of Modern Fiction for Preachers[1]

Extra Lives; Extensions of Empathy; Concrete Imagination

Princeton University, Princeton, New Jersey

There seem to be three values for preachers in the regular reading of outstanding modern fiction. This does not include the desperate hunt for cute or witty anecdotes with which to flavor a sermon which would otherwise be indigestible! These values are: first, an imaginative poet or novelist or dramatist can provide long-term extensions of our lives in both space and time. In this way we will live several lives, past and present, in our own country and in different parts of the world, possibly in five continents. Second, a novel of insight will enlarge our empathy and deepen our compassion, and may even widen our range of humor. Third, a novelist can vivify our words. One of the besetting sins of preaching is using abstractions, not concrete examples. God did not send us a conclusive message until he came as the God-man, Christ, thus visiting and redeeming his people. His messengers need visible words, not wraithlike, and ghostly words: words that have become concretized. Otherwise, why did our Lord teach in parables? Let me exemplify each of these claims with notable examples of the craft of fiction in our day.

Novelists give us extra lives. If we take our context in the United States for granted, where we are free to proclaim the gospel in all its prophetic parameters, then we should read Graham Greene's[2] superb account of the

---

1. See Horton Davies, *A Mirror of the Ministry in Modern Novels*.
2. Graham Greene (1904–1991), English author.

The Value of Modern Fiction for Preachers

brandy priest operating illegally in an officially atheistic Mexico. Greene's *The Power and the Glory* shows us a man who is both the police's wanted man and God's chosen man in a double hunt. He began his ministry as a pampered priest, one of the elite; he ended as one of the elect. Greene's theological mystery exhibits a man who became a saint without knowing it, and at the same time demonstrated what the role of God's servants would be in a world where Caesar, the totalitarian dictator, would increasingly act with all the prerogatives of God.

This is an apocalyptic lesson.

Or, let us suppose, that we have strong theological prejudices, and like superior liberals we insist that the fundamentalists are to be explained as finding the "fun" in "damning the mental." What we need is the marvelous empathy that enables that gifted Presbyterian minister and novelist, Frederick Buechner,[3] to get beneath the skin of Bebb, that apparent con man and cheapjack who runs a theological diploma mill providing certificates of ordination for five dollars a time. Buechner has provided a four-novel study of such in his *The Book of Bebb*, which includes *Lion Country* (this novel was nominated for the National Book Award), *Open Heart* (the appropriate name for the universalist Gospel Church Bebb founded), *Love Feast* (a wonderful romp of a book superbly illustrating confession and forgiveness), and *Treasure Hunt* (with poisonous bitterness contrasted with the surprises that make life joyful). No cardboard figures here, and it is the skeptical agnostic and narrator of the novels who eventually overcomes his prejudice to see the worth of the evangelist Bebb.

An equally effective way of exploding one's own sense of superiority would be provided by reading Peter De Vries's[4] *The Mackerel Plaza*, which is the hilarious account of the minister of the People's Liberal Church in Connecticut, a culture-accommodating parson and church if ever there was one. The Reverend Mr. Mackerel at the outset of the novel is shown phoning the town office to protest against the distraction caused, when he is writing his ten-minute sermon, by an evangelical sign, flashing "Jesus Saves! Jesus Saves!" De Vries is a master of irony when he allows Mackerel to take us round the first split-level community church in the U.S.A. This almost totally horizontal church, without vertical relationship to God, is superbly satirized by its architectural arrangements: downstairs a dining area, kitchen, and three parlors for committee meetings, and upstairs an

---

3. Frederick Buechner (1926-).
4. Peter De Vries (1910–1993).

auditorium for plays, a ballroom for dances, and a gymnasium for athletics. Finally, and almost apologetically, we are informed that there is a small worship area at one end:

> This has a platform cantilevered on both sides, with a freeform pulpit designed by Noguchi. It consists of a slab of marble set on four legs of four delicately differing fruitwoods, to symbolize the four gospels, and their failure to harmonize. Behind it dangles a large multi-colored mobile, its interdenominational parts swaying ... in perpetual reminder of the Pauline stricture against "those blown by every wind of doctrine.[5]

We may laugh at this Hemingway of the pulpit, but if we are totally unreconstructed fundamentalists, the laughs in this book could also be at our expense.

For De Vries is equally critical of the preaching that seems to be only incantation without thought, as well as of repeating slogans. The former weakness is pilloried in the following, "Jesus is the power-house! Are you plugged in? Jesus is the transformer! Are you wired up? Jesus is the cable carrying that current from God Almighty! Is your trolley on?"

As for laughing at slogans, Mackerel has a ready answer for the enthusiast who buttonholes him with the urgent cry, "Brother, have you found Christ?" His facetious riposte is "Is he lost again?"

Whatever the brand of one's theology, it is important both to keep one's sense of humor and to recall that we have not penetrated the mystery of God's innermost thoughts. Thus a satirical novelist can teach us humility and proportion.[6]

If we fail to realize how a charismatic and even corybantic form of Christianity is able to provide reassurance and even joy in an economic and racial ghetto, then we should read James Baldwin's[7] marvelously imaginative novel located in Harlem and see how a sensitive adolescent reaches conversion in a store-front church. This is the experience James Baldwin provides in *Go, Tell it on the Mountain*, which is also a superb evocation of the flowering of young love.

If we are myopic and short-sighted in our provincialism, then one way of getting rid of our northern superiority over the Southerners is to read

---

5. Peter De Vries, *The Mackerel Plaza* (Boston: Little, Brown and Company, 1958), pp. 7–8.

6. "Humility and proportion"—and humor, too: the admonition of Davies.

7. James Baldwin (1924–1987), American novelist.

the brilliant short stories of Flannery O'Connor,[8] that splendid Georgia peach of a writer who died at age thirty-nine from disseminated lupus. She is entirely misunderstood if read as a Roman Catholic author poking fun at grotesque southern Protestant freak characters. She insists that her task as a Christian interpreter is made the easier because the Bible is still the informing story of the South, which gives it its values, even when they are refused. And the characters whom she really despises are the liberals and nihilists, with only a God-shaped blank in their minds, who, as social workers like Sheppard, think of themselves as the Good Shepherd. But Sheppard drives his motherless son to suicide in the story, "The Lame Shall Enter First."[9] Such grotesqueness as she finds is her way of indicating the universal need of redemption for those misshapen by original sin.

If we are Southerners with an assumption that God is white, then we need to get perspective by facing a similar, even more difficult racial situation in another country. This we can find in that Christian parable of Alan Paton,[10] *Cry, the Beloved Country*. This demonstrates in moving terms how Christian faith drives out fear, as it tells how the son of a black Episcopal priest has to hang for the murder of a reformer who had devoted his life to African penal improvement, and how the white father of the reformer and the black priest-father find consolation in mutual forgiveness, because each is conscious of being forgiven by God, and both determine to work for the improvement of inter-ethnic relations in their tragically divided land of South Africa. Here is a powerful retelling of the parable of the Prodigal son.

Novelists do not only give us other lives in our own country and abroad (as we have seen in Mexico and South Africa), but they can take us backwards on the time machine historically. Perhaps the greatest novel that Frederick Buechner has written does exactly this. It is *Godric*, the life of a twelfth-century saint, who was a pirate who robbed pilgrims on their way to Jerusalem and other sacred sites. After a stiff regimen of fasting and contemplation following his conversion, he became a holy hermit. What is so marvelous about this book, which I believe is destined to become an American classic, is that it is written in a lyrical prose, in which the rhythm and shining imagery are all poetry.[11] As on a magic carpet we are trans-

---

8. Flannery O'Connor (1925–1964), American writer.

9. Flannery O'Connor, *The Complete Stories* (New York: Farrar, Strauss and Giroux, 1971), pp. 357–382.

10. Alan Paton (1903–1988), South African writer.

11. This is exactly right: "Only once did he do me a bad turn, and that was from love

ported into the medieval world with its violence and vitality, its tyrannical lords and domineering worldly bishops, but also with its tender love to the Virgin, and its following of Christ and his Cross. Moreover, it forces us to see the importance of the Communion of Saints and to recognize the discipline of the first-class Christians in Roman Catholicism who follow the counsels of perfection, demanding chastity, poverty, and obedience. It is a remarkable Protestant attempt to get under the habit and into the habits of a medieval saint, by one whose own Protestantism is never in doubt. And this particular novel takes us to another country (the north of England in the neighborhood of Durham), to another century (the twelfth), and to another very different interpretation of the life of a Christian (a Catholic hermit).[12]

In the second place, the gifted novelist can provide the preacher with extensions of our empathy. Graham Greene once said in an interview that the aim of most of his novels had been to try to understand what it is to be an outcast. Wasn't that one of the glories of the ministry of Jesus Christ who appreciated the misfits of society? He commended the wit of the Syro-Phoenician woman, accepted water from the woman of Samaria, had his cross carried by an African Simon of Cyrene, made a disciple of Matthew, the loathed tax-gatherer for the Romans, promised salvation to a crucified thief, and promised that a prostitute who bathed his feet with her tears and dried them with her hair, should always be remembered because she had anticipated his burial honorably. It is the glory of St. Luke's gospel that he shows the sublime compassion of Jesus, not the pity of a superior, but the equality of a sufferer.

Part of our terrible apathy and indifference is due to our lack of imagination. And perhaps the finest sentence in Greene's *The Power and the Glory* is that which says, "Hatred is a failure of the imagination." A pharisaic old lady in a Mexican jail is condemning two young people for making love in that prison where otherwise hatred abounds; that is a situation in which this profound statement of Greene is made. And in our routinized,

---

as many a bad turn's been done from before"—Frederick Buechner, *Godric* (New York: Atheneum, 1981), p. 6. Put those words next to the words of Father Zosima: "... love in action is a harsh and dreadful thing compared with love in dreams"—Fyodor Dostoevsky, *The Brothers Karamazov*, trans. Constance Garnett, revised Abraham Yarmolinsky (New York: The Heritage Press, 1933), p. 41.

12. See Marie-Hélène Davies, *Laughter in a Genevan Gown: The Works of Frederick Buechner, 1970–1980* (Grand Rapids, Michigan: Eerdmans, 1983) for a full analysis of Buechner's literary technique.

dry-as-dust, conventional world, it is often only the novelist who can enable us to see beneath the rusty exterior of coin the image of the king of kings.

Imagination is what we are in need of, and this is the gift of the supreme artists of the word. In order to cultivate compassion we need to overcome the "balcony view" of life and to get down into the dust and combat characteristic of the "arena view" of life. This our novelists can do for us. Camus, a brilliant agnostic whose ethics reveal the Catholicism which he gave up but which never entirely left him, demonstrates this in his novel, *The Fall*, the story of a man who is haunted by the drowning cry of a woman who fell from a bridge into the Seine in Paris, and whom he never attempted to rescue.

We should also avoid the himalayan, above-it-all attitude which is that of the chief character in William Golding's[13] novel, *The Spire*. He is the Dean of Salisbury cathedral, England, in the fourteenth century, who has determined to build the loftiest spire in the kingdom. In theory the chief motive was for the glory of God; in reality it was at least in part for the glory of the Dean. We see him drive the master builder who is afraid of heights, and who has excavated the earth beneath the crossing and found the foundations utterly unsound, upwards far beyond his safety and the safety of his workers. The Dean's domineering will makes the rest of the cathedral unsafe, so that divine worship has to take place for smaller congregations elsewhere, and the Dean is too busy to pray. His ambition and superiority to the advice of his confessor makes him inhuman until he almost destroys himself and his charges. His basic lack is compassion, forgetting that God has had compassion on him. We assume that he receives absolution at the last, after he has sought the forgiveness of others whom he has ruined. This novel is an unforgettable parable about the necessity of compassion in a servant of God, and the higher his rank and responsibility, the greater the need for it.

Compassion is also linked with humility. Flannery O'Connor's story, "The Enduring Chill" makes this clear. It is concerned with a know-it-all college graduate, Asbury. He is superior to his mother and his sister the headmistress, knows more about religion than Father Finn, and more about medicine than Dr. Block, and intends to teach his mother a lesson that will bring her an enduring chill on his death. But his arrogance begins to crack

---

13. William Golding (1911–1993), English author. He won the Nobel Prize in Literature in 1993.

and the Holy Spirit appears to him like a chilling and terrifying bird on the wall of his bedroom that chills him to a freezing humility.[14]

I would want to argue that, just as the sense of community among Christians of any different denominations has been created in part by the need to fight the common and increasingly powerful enemy of nihilistic atheism, so we need a wider ecumenism in which Christian ministers in particular have a responsibility to understand other religions empathetically. The first priority here must be to understand the faith of Judaism from which Christianity emerged, for which compassion (*cheseth*) is a predominant virtue. The more we know about the Holocaust, the more easily can we be rid of the poison of anti-Semitism and cultivate a profound empathy for Judaism and the Jews. Here again the novelists can come to our rescue.

The two interpreters of Judaism that I find most helpful are Chaim Potok[15] and Elie Wiesel.[16] For a documentary account of what it is like to have your mother and sister go to the gas ovens, and your father to die beside you on a murderous journey towards liberation from which you are among the pathetically few survivors, read Wiesel's *Night*. If you want to know what it is like in a supposedly Christian country to survive the persecution or indifference of your neighbors, read Wiesel's *The Gates of the Forest*. There you will realize that the Jewish adolescent Gregor (using a non-Jewish name) survives for some years only because he is thought to be deaf and dumb! If you wish to understand the difference between the strict Hasidic sect and the Conservative Jews, then read Chaim Potok's *The Chosen* and you will understand why the Hasidim above all fear to assimilate, and why the Conservatives are committed to creating a haven republic for Jews in Israel as Zionists.

For introductions to Buddhism, profoundly a religion of compassion, it should be noted I recommend Takeyama's[17] *The Harp of Burma*, where the hero is the perfect exemplar of the arena view of life. A former Japanese soldier who has sacrificed his safety for his friends while fighting in Burma, decides to stay on in that land while the other prisoners-of-war are repatriated. He wishes to bury the corpses of all the Japanese comrades who died in Burma, sensing that their souls are uneasy unburied. He was the man who risked his life to persuade another company of Japanese soldiers to

---

14. Flannery O'Connor, *The Complete Stories*, pp. 357–382.
15. Chaim Potok, *My Name Is Asher Lev* (New York: Alfred A. Knopf, 1972).
16. Elie Wiesel (1928-).
17. Michio Takeyama (1903–1984), Japanese author and scholar of German literature.

surrender because the war was over, although they had not known it in their isolated field position. In a supreme act of ecumenical compassion he, now wearing the ochre garb of a Buddhist monk, placed a ruby on the memorial of the British dead in the Second World War.

A third value of novelists (or poets for that matter) for the preacher is that they help us make our words in communicating the Word of God far less abstract and much more vivid and concrete. Let us suppose that a sermon is being prepared on the double aspect of the nature of God as holy (and therefore distant from us) and merciful (and near to us). These are abstract concepts, but how they have become etched on our memories, or focused on the retina of our imagination, in these lines from Gerard Manley Hopkins's *The Wreck of the Deutschland*, "Thou art lightning and love, I found it, a winter and warm."[18]

It is worth remembering that many of our novelists were also able painters, drawers, or caricaturists, such as D. H. Lawrence, John Updike, and Frederick Buechner. Among the poets, the painters include Blake, D. G. Rossetti, and Edward Lear, to take only a few examples. Artists in words can only convey their thoughts if they can enable their audience to visualize them. God, the creator of the rainbow and the rose, assures us through the Letter to the Colossians that Christ is "the image of the invisible God" (the Greek word is *ikōn*). Perhaps it is St. Athanasius in his *Concerning the Incarnation*[19] who best expresses the purpose of God enabling us to visualize him in Christ. Athanasius, that adamantly Orthodox theologian, says that Christ came from heaven to confront us at our own level and height so that we could not miss him in wild guesses, or, as Charles Wesley[20] understood it, God "contracted to a span / Most marvelously ["Incomprehensibly"] made man."[21]

That is why the preacher needs vividness, and that craft is developed by osmosis through frequent reading of the best craftsmen and craftswomen of words in our language, the novelists, dramatists and poets. They will cultivate our imagination and enable us to be vivid image-makers. Suppose the minister wishes to produce a sermon on greed; which is often the problem of members of well-heeled suburban churches. He could do no

---

18. Gerard Manley Hopkins, "The Wreck of the Deutschland," ed. Oscar Williams, *A Little Treasury of Modern Poetry* (New York: Charles Scribner's Sons, 1952), p. 29, IX.
19. *De Incarnatione Verbi Dei.*
20. Charles Wesley (1707-1788).
21. "Let Earth and Heaven Combine" (1745).

better in pointing out the utter inhumanity of our living on a superfluity of food while nations in Southeast Asia and parts of Africa are dying from malnutrition than read and retell the stories in Graham Greene's mystery novel, *Dr. Fischer, Or, the Geneva Bomb Plot*, or William Golding's *Pincher Martin*, or Flannery O'Connor's story, "A View of the Woods." The first tells of the wealthy friends of Dr. Fischer who are invited at regular intervals to his home, where they will crawl in their eagerness to receive his fabulous presents, even though they need none of them, and the price they must pay is extreme humiliation at their host's caustic tongue. So rapacious are they that finally they even risk their lives for their greed. Similarly, Pincher Martin, so we are told, went through life "with his mouth and his fly always open." O'Connor's story tells of a high-handed grandfather who sells the land in front of his son-in-law's house for a gas station to be built upon it, although this destroys the family's view. His cupidity challenged by his honest granddaughter, results eventually in his murdering her for her impudent independence. The same type of theme is elaborated in George Eliot's[22] famous study of a miser, *Silas Marner*. After reading any of these stories greed is no longer an abstraction, but a wolf-like maw and an elastic stomach.

If we wish to convey the seriousness of hypocrisy, which derives from a Greek word for play-acting and implies dissimulation, it will not be enough to suggest a mask. This is because few modern actors wear masks. Our Lord's condemnation of hypocrites as "whited sepulchers" is certainly striking, pointing to a glistening exterior hiding a rotting interior. But "sepulchers" are anachronistic today. If we want to see the destructive impact of hypocrisy in action, we can visualize it in the character and actions of Brigitte Pian in Nobel Prize Winner, François Mauriac's[23] *A Woman of the Pharisees*. Her charitable acts reduced others to total subservience to her. Her jealousy of a highly intelligent priest in the neighborhood caused him to lose his theological professorship and ultimately even the right to celebrate the sacraments because she reported him to the archbishop as unreliable in doctrine and character. This is hypocrisy alive and all too well.

For vividness, Updike is hard to beat. Consider the following account of early dawn, painted with the bright acrylic colors of an artist's palette[24]:

---

22. George Eliot, pen name of Mary Anne Evans (1819–1880).

23. Francois Mauriac (1885–1970) received the Nobel Prize in Literature in 1952. He is instrumental in encouraging the writing career of Elie Wiesel.

24. Horton Davies knows well "the bright acrylic colors of an artist's palette." HD.

The Value of Modern Fiction for Preachers

"Despite the low orange sun, still wet from its dawning, crescents of mist like the webs of tent caterpillars adhered in the crotches of the hills."[25] The image is perfect and the word "crotch" by its unusualness grabs our attention. Finally, as an example of the unforgettable, apt, and witty modem parallel of a logion of Jesus, there is Buechner's illustration of it, "Easier for Nelson Rockefeller to pass through the night deposit slot of the Chase Manhattan Bank"[26] as the equivalent for "It is easier for a camel to pass through the eye of a needle than for a rich man to enter the kingdom of God" [Matthew 19:24; Mark 10:25; Luke 18:25]. This, of itself, is proof how an unusually gifted novelist mints new images and words to make his meaning memorable. We can all learn from such expertise in communication how to convey the gospel compellingly, and at the same time vividly.

---

25. John Updike (1932–2009), *The Poorhouse Fair*, 7. This remarkable novel, Updike's earliest [1959], shows an astonishing ability on the part of the young man to understand the values and psychology of the aged. Written in 1957, it was supposed to take place in 1977 (HD).

26. Frederick Buechner, *Peculiar Treasures. A Biblical Who's Who.* (New York: Harper and Row, 1979), preface.

Worship and the Renewal of the Church
Christian Art. The Holiness of Beauty
Brookfield Congregational Church, Connecticut, 1959.

Tonight, I face a great difficulty. You have come to hear me talk about "Christian Art. The Holiness of Beauty," and I have to confess that where I have found great Christian architecture and great Christian art in the twentieth century is not in the Protestant Churches: it is in the Roman Catholic Church, or in the Anglican Church. So what am I to do? Am I to spend this precious time with you lamenting the staleness of our imitative church architecture, repeating a stale Gothic medievalism that is as irrelevant as a gargoyle in twentieth century architecture? Am I to decry our color-blind sanctuaries in Protestantism, which seem to declare that they believe in the full inspiration of the local decorator, or proclaim, "I believe in geometry, but not in God," because they have no reference to the mighty acts of God in our salvation, being empty of images or representations of the Virgin Mary cradling her blessed son, or of the climactic act of our salvation, the Cross, or of the glory of the resurrection and the extension of man's life beyond the muddy confines of the grave?

But this would be only to pour salt on old wounds. I am going to take the positive way of sharing with you my appreciation of some examples of creative art and architecture. It will prove, I hope, that, in the present century, great interpretative Christian art in architecture, painting, stained-glass windows, and sculpture, is actually being made in days that the cynics call the post-Christian age.[1] I hope that after this service is over, you will walk in the adjacent room to your right, and see the three representations about which I am now to speak.

---

1. See Horton Davies and Hugh Davies, *Sacred Art in a Secular Century*.

Architecture

One can say with confidence that the trend of modern church architecture is away from the monumentally massive, theatrical cathedral to the simple, domestic and functional type of building. In brief, we are moving from the fortress of God to the most transitory symbol of the tent of God. The fortress of God was altogether suitable for the cathedrals of the Middle Ages, that great age of faith, when the church was at the heart of the life of the people and was the very center of its city life. There was one denomination, not many. The church was not only a worship center, but also school, center for drama, psychiatric clinic, meeting place for all the guilds of craftsmen, each of which had its own chapel. Even the annual fair, if the weather was dry, was held on the square in front of the West door, and, if wet, inside the cathedral. No wonder these medieval cathedrals tower over the ancient cities of Europe, like a hen gathering in the chickens of cottages about it, in Chartres, York, or Durham. And the worship inside it was a spectator's worship. Those great vaulted naves carried the eye along to the central altar, where an offended God was propitiated by the sacrifice of the Mass, offered by the distant priesthood in a mysterious tongue, and accompanied by a choir. The people were silent spectators, kept back from the central holy place by screens and steps.

But the Reformation changed all that: Luther and Calvin[2] discovered that man did not have to appease an irate deity, but that a loving God had come in search of men,[3] in Jesus Christ who had invited them to share his holy Banquet, the Lord's Supper. In listening to the preaching of the Word, in all joining and singing the hymns, and especially as guests of the Lord's table, they were participants, sharers. And so the two-roomed mighty cathedral—choir, and nave and distant altar—were changed into a single room, in which the pulpit and the table were given the central position.

In our day, an imposing cathedral seems all wrong. It is too domineering a symbol for a faith that must fight to gain a hearing; too stable for the rapid social change of today and the movement of populations; too unsuitable for a democratically shared worship. And instead, the more suitable modern symbol is a tent of pilgrimage for God's people, without ornate or permanent fixtures. It is interesting that the most notable expression of the tent symbol is that provided by the Protestant architect of the new Roman

2. John Calvin (1509–1564).
3. See n. 12, p. 20 above.

Catholic Cathedral at Liverpool, Frederick Gibberd.[4] The outside looks exactly like a vast tent, surmounted by a cylinder and a crown, to symbolize the lordship of the crucified Christ with the crown of thorns. The interior is a completely circular sanctuary with a central altar so constructed that three thousand people can be within seventy feet of the steps leading to the altar. It says compellingly to all worshippers two things: here we have no abiding city for we seek a heavenly one [Hebrews 13:14]; this is our tent of pilgrimage. It also says: the center of our lives is the crucified Christ, and, in this circle, we are all brethren.

Our day has seen the most remarkable technical changes in architecture, so that prestressed concrete can be molded in almost any shape you can think of. And this is the reason why Christianity must use the new materials and new shapes instead of harking back to imitations of Gothic, and seeming irrelevant to our times. Presbyterians who go anywhere near Stamford, Connecticut, should make a point of seeing the Presbyterian Church in that city. It is almost entirely made of glass, with the most marvelous rainbow hues and colors, really expressive of the Creator God.

Christian Art

I want to spend the rest of our time indicating how some major artists have given new life and meaning to the great Christian themes. The architect of Coventry cathedral, Sir Basil Spence,[5] was able to secure the services of some of the most famous artists of the day. Therefore Coventry has become a jeweled casket of modern Christian Art; so let us look at this widely published cathedral first, the fortress of Coventry:

The cathedral has many remarkable features. First its shape is zigzag, so that it looks like an accordion on the sides. As you enter by the great west door of solid glass on which angels and the great saints of Britain are inscribed, you cannot see a single window inside. But when you reach the high altar and look back at the west door, it is a sheet of multi-colored glass on either side. The colors of the glass are supposed to represent the symbolism of various stages of life: green and yellow stand for youth; pink and red stand for passion and adolescence; then multi-colored stand for experience; then deep blue and purple stand for wisdom; and finally gold, standing for the serenity of old age and the hope of the resurrection.

    4. Frederick Gibberd (1908–1984), English architect.
    5. Sir Basil Unwin Spence (1907–1976), Scottish architect.

Worship and the Renewal of the Church

On your left is the chapel of Unity, shaped like a crusader's tent. Opposite it is a coruscating window of almost two hundred different mullioned lights, the famous baptistery window of John Piper.[6] On the south side, near the altar, is an adjoining chapel: the chapel of Christ the servant, which is all translucent glass and shines out in the night. Like a cheering lighthouse, this is the industrial chaplaincy of Coventry, a smaller Detroit and center of car-manufacture. The building is remarkable in its own right. But I want to concentrate on three of its works of Christian art.

The whole of the east wall of the cathedral is filled by the largest tapestry in the world, in glorious green and gold, woven in France, to the designs of Graham Sutherland.[7] This is over seventy-five feet high and thirty-eight feet wide. Its subject is Christ in glory. This shows a serenely young and compassionate Christ, with both hands raised in blessing. Yet the nail-prints are seen in his feet, between which stands typical man in the erect position, to which Christ has raised our fallen humanity. Christ's simple white, monk-like garment swells out in egg-wide shape, accented by yellow tints on the white from waist to knees. This egg-like shape suggests that Christ is the recreate and regenerative principle, by whom we receive the new life of the Spirit. Around him are the symbols of the four evangelists, excitedly witnessing to his victory over the powers of sin and death and suffering. But the marvel is that when you come close to the tapestry, you find that the lower third of it paints a very different picture, for this panel turns out to be a most moving and stark representation of Christ's crucifixion, exhibiting a pallid, emaciated and tortured Christ. Its blacks and grays strike the right somber notes of the Christ who passed to his glory through the anguish and desolation of the Cross. It cries out, "was ever sorrow like my sorrow," and bids the complaining Christian be still.

The second great work of art in the cathedral at Coventry is, of course, the immense, glowing, jeweled wonder of John Piper's baptistery window, the marvel of which is that it keeps thousands guessing as to its meaning because it is abstract art relying on its effect entirely by its color. It is made out of one hundred and ninety-eight different panes of glass. It is flanked by crimson hues, but the eye is first caught by the central circle of pure white light, ringed with gold, which leads above into bands of a dark sepia that merge into an irregular rectangle of bewitching butterfly blue, deepening into purple at the edges, in turn leading to the crimson of the border. Here

6. John Egerton Christmas Piper (1903–1992), English artist.
7. Graham Sutherland (1903–1980), English artist.

and there, the lights are flecked with brilliant gold. Below, the white circle ringed with gold merges into fresh bracken green, then into light sepia and it reaches the base in aquamarine tints. There on an octagonal plinth of black marble, rests an enormous hollowed out primeval bowl for baptism.

For some, the central white circle edged with gold will resemble a pool, a fitting symbol of the cleansing of baptism, and the impact of the coolness of Christ in life's fever will seem as freshening as plunge into a pool fed by ice-cold mountain cataracts. Others may interpret the white circle like the poet Henry Vaughan[8] who wrote, "I saw eternity the other night, a ring of pure and endless light." That is they may see this ring as the symbol of the endlessness of eternity; and they may interpret the butterfly blue on high as a symbol of the eternal dimension of Christian living. Yet others will link the blue and white as the virginal colors of chastity and perfection. The greatness of the window is that it reminds us of the glory of God's creation, on the one hand, and, on the other, of that new life in Christ of which the beginning is baptism.

The third great work of art is on the outside wall of the Cathedral, the work of a brilliant Brooklyn-born sculptor, Sir Jacob Epstein,[9] this marvelous Jew who is perhaps the greatest 20th century interpreter of Christian symbols. This massive work weighs four tons; it is a bronze sculpture of *St. Michael's Victory over the Devil* (1958). St. Michael is the patron saint of Coventry. The figure of St. Michael is nineteen feet and six inches high and the span of his wings extends to twenty-three feet. Below him, the devil lies chained in defeat. In the dedication service of the Epstein group, the Bishop of Coventry said of the representation of the devil, "Here is no stupid melodramatic portrayal of an unreal entity; here is a man, fallen man, man as we see him today, man who has cast himself out of heaven." He went on to describe Sir Jacob Epstein, who died in 1959, the year before the unveiling, as "a very great artist, a man much misunderstood, a giant who had to face the jibes and the jeers of the little men."

The strong group is a powerful image of the eternal struggle between good and evil, giving and grasping attitudes to life. It seems as if St. Michael stands for the athlete of the spirit, poised and ready to do the divine bidding, ever vigilant. The devil is shown as paunchy, heavy, groveling, and the symbol of selfish indulgence. The force of the group derives from a contrast. The angel has a vertical up thrust, with pillar-like body and upright spear,

---

8. Henry Vaughan (1621–1695), Welsh writer and poet.
9. See n. 3, p. 166 above.

all austerity and aspiration and freedom, as the extended arms and feet suggest. This up thrust contrasts with the down drag of the proud and sensual devil, with his heavy thighs and paunch, his barrel-chest, his arrogant bull-like head. He is still writhing, tough bound, the rebel against God still protesting with his jutting impudent chin and the splayed fingers twisted behind his back. There is the double paradox: God's servant is free, but the libertine is enslaved. It is a great work of art on a central Christian theme of the spiritual civil war within us.

I want to close by describing one other work of Christian art achieved by that genuine Epstein. It is *The Madonna and Child*, a masterpiece in lead that hangs on the exterior of the walls of the Convent of the Holy Child Jesus, in Cavendish Square in the heart of London's west end. I shall cite the words of the poet Laurie Lee[10] to try to do justice to it in words:

> The setting is perfect. The two figures float above us with no apparent artifice of support. The Christ Child is not the customary babe but a lean boy of some five or six years. The mantled Mother with open hands reveals and offers him to the world. And the child, both in expression and design, is all prophecy; the robe that wraps his narrow body is also the robe of the tomb; the arms outstretched to embrace the world also assume the attitude of crucifixion; and the face with its large white eyes and serene brow, looks out with love and knows what love will cost him. This is one of the finest, most subtle, most affectionate of Epstein's works. It is also one of the most original conceptions of its theme.

God knew that we mortals would be lost in guesses about his nature in abstractions. So he came in the flesh in Jesus Christ, the image of invisible God. And we may thank God that when so many crude, sensational, and degrading images of the meaning of humanity are projected in the films and on the television screens of our day, that great artists are combating them by showing us, like Epstein, Sutherland, Henry Moore, Georges Rouault, and John Piper, the ever-relevant image of God in Christ.

Let us pray:

O God, who hast shown us in the life of thy saints the beauty of holiness and in thy artists the holiness of beauty, keep us alert to both visions of thyself. Forgive us for the willful blindness that condemns all modern art because it

---

10. Lawrence Edward Alan "Laurie" Lee (1914–1997), English author.

How Far Down Dare I Drink?

is modern and would compel all artists to repeat the stale styles of the past to suit our sentimentality. Give us sympathetic eyes to discern new glories in the imaginations of the architects and artists of today that we may think creative thoughts through them. Make us alive to the color and glory of the universe as seen anew in their eyes; make us sensitive to the ugliness of the universe, that man-made ugliness of slums and exploitation and shoddy workmanship, which prophetic artists force us to see in their deliberate depictions of it. Above all, grant us to build sanctuaries for thy worship which shall express not the grimness and gloom of unredeemed spirits, but the joy and glory of those who know and share the love of Christ, who said "Consider the lilies of the field; they toil not, neither do they weep; yet Solomon in all his glory is not arrayed like one of these" [Matthew 18:28–29; Luke 12:27]. Give us, then, as thy witnesses, the beauty of holiness and the holiness of beauty, through Jesus Christ our Lord. Amen.

Pilgrimage
Eden Lost and Emmaus Found
An American Sermon, c. 1980

Pilgrimage: what does the word conjure up in your minds? . . . Perhaps the Pilgrims of 1620 who, in that cockleshell of a boat, the *Mayflower*, crossed the Atlantic with their covenanted families in a voyage that tried and tested faith. Or perhaps we think of the very hymnal that we use, called *The Pilgrim Hymnal*. Or it may be the prose epic of Puritanism, John Bunyan's *Pilgrim's Progress*, as the poetic epic was *Paradise Lost*.[1] Or, possibly you have in mind the jovial fourteenth century company, the Canterbury Pilgrims who traveled to Canterbury for fun's sake, and for faith's, the "holy martyr for to seke," Saint Thomas à Becket.[2] Or you recall Malcolm X's[3] *Autobiography*, when this black American joined the millions of Muslims on the journey to Mecca, and found a genuine and moving brotherhood that he had never before experienced, and which was more than skin deep, but God-deep.

For my wife, Helen, and I who have spent two summers [1974–1975] traveling through the four pilgrimage roads through France to northwestern Spain, marking the huge abbeys and cathedrals that were way-stations to the great medieval shrine of Compostela, pilgrimage means a book that is called *Holy Days and Holidays: The Medieval Pilgrimage to Compostela*.[4] But even more, it was through the iconography, studying the carved and

---

1. John Milton (1608–1674), *Paradise Lost* (1664).
2. St. Thomas à Becket (c. 1118–1170), Archbishop of Canterbury, 1162–1170.
3. Malcolm X (1925–1965).
4. Horton and Marie-Hélène Davies, *Holy Days and Holidays: The Medieval Pilgrimage to Compostela* (Lewisburg, Pennsylvania: Bucknell University Press, 1982).

painted images on the way, that we sensed how frequently the Bible depicts the theme of pilgrimage.

Adam was a reluctant pilgrim, expelled from paradise; God's ancient chosen people, the Jews, went on a forty year pilgrimage from the slavery of Egypt to the liberation of Canaan; Joseph and Mary were to reverse the journey with the infant Jesus, going to Egypt to avoid the Massacre of the Innocents [see Matthew 2:16]; the three magi bringing their tributes to the infant Lord were pilgrims; the most fantastic pilgrimage of all was the journey of Christ through death to everlasting life, and the strangest pilgrimage, a pilgrimage of despair to hope, the experience of the two Emmaus pilgrims [see Luke 24:13–35]. In any case, pilgrims are distinguished from tourists in having a sacred aim and purpose, a holy direction in their lives.

For all Christians life is a pilgrimage: a journey through all the changing scenes of life, short or long, sometimes alone; for we begin and end that journey alone, but most of the time, we are accompanied by family and friends; and for everyone, it means climbing the Hill of Difficulty and often falling into the Slough of Despond [*The Pilgrim's Progress*].

Frederick Buechner, a Princeton graduate of the English department, of the class of 1947, has provided a superb map of the way in his Lyman Beecher lectures at Yale University, called *Telling the Truth: The Gospel as Tragedy, Comedy, and Fairy Tale*.[5]

Eden Lost

I think there is not one of us who has not had the experience of Adam, with a sense of a lost Eden, where the way back to paradise is barred, with the cherubim and an angel with a drawn sword guarding the way [see Genesis 3:24]. Have we not, at some stage of our life, sensed paradise lost, a place where we would be truly at home, where no one would feel a stranger, unloved and unclean, wanting to be forgiven and understood? We are like the Prodigal son; we have been disobedient, and even if we have not wasted our substance in riotous living, the world has been too much with us; getting and spending, we have laid waste our powers; our spirits have shriveled, and we want desperately to find our way home because, foolish son, or foolish daughter, we have at last come to ourselves. And God our Father, as our Lord assures us, is waiting to welcome us back home; forgiveness is in

---

5. Davies uses Buechner's original title: *Telling the Truth: The Gospel as Tragedy, Comedy and the Fairy Tale That Is True* (San Francisco: Harper & Row, Publishers, 1977).

Pilgrimage

the gesture of his outstretched arms and in the command to call and make merry, for the lost son or daughter is found, and so there must be a feast [see Luke 15:20–24].

Yes, we are all reluctant pilgrims. Yes, we'd love to find the way home. But how... but how?

Emmaus: the Way Home

Our second lesson gives us the clue: Eden is recovered by the way of Emmaus. The two dejected disciples are on their way from Jerusalem, the place where their leader and Lord had been mercilessly liquidated, expiring in a long drawn-out agony in the blistering heat of a merciless sun, between two thieves, one of whom was cursing all the time. For these disciples, this was the bitter end of the promised kingdom of God, of Christ whose mouth had been filled with the dust of the sepulcher. This was the day of the devil's victory, with his leering and sneering, and all the louts of doubt and the lunatics who laugh at God were having their hellish holiday. Then a stranger joined the two disciples. He told them that this was to be expected: the messiah's sacrificial death, and their loneliness, and the trials of their doubt.

He seemed strange and yet, curiously, a little familiar too, and, as they sat at table in the inn, at the end of the day, and as he broke the bread, their eyes could not believe what they saw. The way he broke the bread and blessed it flashed their thoughts back to another meal, the Last Supper, and they recalled that their master had said on that occasion," I will not drink of the fruit of the vine until I drink it new in my Father's kingdom" [Matthew 26:29; Mark 14:25; Luke 22:18]. This meant that the king of kings had come into his kingdom; in Christ's case, death itself was the final victim; he had returned mysteriously to his own.

Let me try to create that flashback with the help of two distinguished artists. One of them is Sir Stanley Spencer[6] of our own century, and the other is the greatest biblical interpreter of them all, Rembrandt van Rijn of the seventeenth century.

Spencer paints *The Last Supper* (1920) on the background of his native Cookham-on-Thames, using an old brick malt house. The dominant colors are red and white, for wine and bread, of course. The disciples are clothed in white robes, and their hoods falling on their backs have a suggestion of wings, hinting that, in the divine empowerment, they will become saints.

---

6. Sir Stanley Spencer (1891–1959), English painter.

How Far Down Dare I Drink?

But the marvelous and unique character of this painting is something that John, the beloved disciple, observes with stupefaction: the loaf just broken in Christ's hands is heart-shaped, and Christ's own heart will be broken on Good Friday in love for the disciples and the world.

Imagine with me now just one of Rembrandt's paintings of *The Inn at Emmaus*. The background is extremely dark, and the dominant color is brown turned ochre by the light that shines through it. A servant has just brought in bread and wine; behind the table is a very compassionate Jesus, and at each side of the table is a disciple. Their eyes are riveted on the hands of Jesus and you can see on their faces the interior drama that is taking place: at first incredulity and doubt, and then astonishment. Finally joy gives way to faith and absolute trust.

And for them all, the promises of Christ ring true, and all the difficulties of the journey dissolve, all the heartaches and headaches dissolve, and they remember the words now proven beyond a shadow of a doubt, "In my Father's house are many mansions: if it were not so, I would have told you. I go to prepare a place that where I am, ye may be also" [John 14:2–3] And his followers in the New Testament and beyond find the way back home, believing that if we suffer with him, we shall also reign with him [see 2 Timothy 2:11–12].

Eden lost may be found again, through the Emmaus experience. So rejoice pilgrims, as you journey towards the sunset that coruscates on the Delectable Mountains [*The Pilgrim's Progress*] and glimpse through the mists of time the shining citadels of eternity, where they hold high festival as souls come, singing, and exulting, home. And he, the prince of peace, puts his wounded arms about your shoulders, saying, "Well done, good and faithful servants; enter into the joy of your Lord" [see Matthew 25:21, 23].

www.ingramcontent.com/pod-product-compliance
Lightning Source LLC
Chambersburg PA
CBHW071230170426
43191CB00032B/1223